FIG TREE JOHN

For Larry —
with deep
appreciation.

Pete

Fig Tree John

FIG TREE JOHN

An Indian in Fact and Fiction

PETER G. BEIDLER

The University of Arizona Press
Tucson, Arizona

About the Author . . .

PETER G. BEIDLER, professor of English at Lehigh University, combines anthropological, historical, and literary research to bring to light two Fig Tree Johns — the factual one who lived in the deserts of southern California, and the fictional one who is the protagonist of Edwin Corle's novel of Apache life, *Fig Tree John*. In 1974 Beidler was a National Endowment for the Humanities Postdoctoral Fellow in the Department of Anthropology at the University of Arizona.

THE UNIVERSITY OF ARIZONA PRESS

Copyright ©1977
The Arizona Board of Regents
All Rights Reserved
Manufactured in the U.S.A.

Library of Congress Cataloging in Publication Data

Beidler, Peter G.
  Fig Tree John

  Bibliography: p.
  Includes index.
  1. Corle, Edwin, 1906–   Fig Tree John.   2. Fig
Tree John, in fiction, drama, poetry, etc.   I.   Title.
PS3505.0669F533   813'.5'2   76-26345
ISBN 0-8165-0600-0
ISBN 0-8165-0522-5 pbk.

For PAUL GORMAN

CONTENTS

ILLUSTRATIONS

FOREWORD

Edwin Corle was a big, hearty, confident man and writer when I first met him in 1951. Our meeting was in the Westwood Bookstore on the edge of the UCLA campus. Ed was a graduate of that university and I was its Librarian. My bibliography of novels with a Southern California setting had recently been published, and it included *Fig Tree John*, with an annotation of high praise for the novel.

And so it was natural for Corle to ask me to write a Foreword for a new edition of *Fig Tree John* to be published by the Ward Ritchie Press, with illustrations by Don Perceval.

That led to my wife and me visiting the Corles at their elegant home on the Hope Ranch in Santa Barbara. While Fay and Jean became acquainted in the big house before lunch, Ed and I talked about books and writing in general and his novel in particular. He had built a separate studio to his own specifications. It housed his working library of upwards of 6,000 volumes. They were shelved around a central desk from which Corle could swivel his chair and seize upon the volume he wanted. He and I shared a love for books and an appreciation of their role in research and writing. He was a fine working bookman, concerned with facts and accuracy. (I am happy to note in passing that his library was given to UCLA by his widow Jean after Ed's untimely death in 1952.)

The letter Corle wrote me, reproduced herein by Peter Beidler, was intended as a summary of our discussion that day in his studio. I was hesitant, as I always am, in contributing a Foreword to another writer's book. I knew that Corle would not like my judgment, then and now, that his first novel, *Fig Tree John,* was his best novel. What prolific writer can accept the implied criticism of his subsequent work? Yet it was true also of Oliver La Farge. He never surpassed *Laughing Boy* and, he said bitterly, it hung around his neck like the albatross for the rest of a life in which he was to write many more books.

Ed Corle would be pleased with this searching critique in which Peter Beidler pays high tribute to a young writer's first major effort. I see it also as a stimulus to similar studies of other writers' use of Indian subjects: *Laughing Boy,* for example, and Will Levington Comfort's *Apache.* Peter Beidler here has demonstrated the necessary combination of skills in literature, anthropology, and history to inspire others as well as himself to like enterprise in this field. So let him go forward. I promise to follow with forewords!

LAWRENCE CLARK POWELL

PREFACE

EVER SINCE JAMES FENIMORE COOPER discovered the richness that American Indian characters can lend to a novel, American writers have been incorporating Indians as either major or minor characters in their short stories and novels. Such diverse writers as Walt Whitman and Ken Kesey, Edgar Allen Poe and Ernest Hemingway, Herman Melville and N. Scott Momaday, Mark Twain and William Faulkner have incorporated Indians into their fiction. Fiction about Indians, however, has attracted relatively little scholarly attention. Historians tend to think of Indians in fiction as mere hack popularizations of mistaken impressions; anthropologists tend to scoff at the crude errors novelists make in dealing with Indian life; literary critics have become so conditioned to expecting the same old stereotypes of the noble son of the forest, the scalping savage, the drunken half-wit, the sad victim of white domination, the thwarted conservationist, that few of them take fiction about Indians very seriously. Although this scholarly neglect of fiction dealing with Indians is often deserved, we should guard against letting the many bad novelists and novels ruin it for the few good ones.

Even though much of it has been of questionable literary quality, fiction dealing with Indians has been influential. Because many people have learned most of what they know (or think they know) about Indians through fiction,

it is important to try to determine which fictional represen-
tations of Indians are most reliable. It is also important to
consider to what extent fiction even *can* be factually accurate
in its portrayal of Indians, as well as what its limitations
and advantages are as a medium for conveying information
about them.

In trying to find the beginnings of answers to these
kinds of questions, I have examined how one serious novelist handled factual materials in one novel. I selected Edwin
Corle as the novelist, because I knew that he was sincerely
interested in Indians and had written several novels about
them. I selected his first novel, *Fig Tree John* (1935), for
concentrated study, because it is generally considered to be
his best novel, and because I knew it was inspired by facts.
I found that the factual elements Corle had worked from
were still traceable some years after the novelist himself
was dead, and many years after the historical model for his
main character was dead. With a little luck and a lot of help,
I was able to track down the background materials which
were to form the basis of my study of the relationship
between the facts of an Indian's life and culture and the fictional representation of that life and culture in the work of
a serious novelist. The results of that search, and the implications of it, led to this book.

ACKNOWLEDGMENTS

I OWE THANKS to the National Endowment for the Humanities for a fellowship which enabled me to spend a year at the University of Arizona, learning what I could about Indians in life and in literature; to the staff at the Department of Anthropology and the libraries of the University of Arizona for leading me to a great deal of factual information about southwestern Indians; to Lowell John Bean, Department of Anthropology, California State University at Hayward, to Harry W. Lawton, Department of Anthropology, University of California in Riverside, to Arthur Sonneborn, Editor of the *Indio Daily News,* to Ole Nordland of the Coachella Valley Historical Society, to Brooke Whiting of the UCLA Research Library, to the staff at the Bureau of Indian Affairs agency at Riverside, and to Harry C. James, for helping me to locate materials on Fig Tree John; to the Coachella Valley residents whose names appear in my bibliography (especially to Louisa Aguilar, to Jane Penn, and to Cecilia Foulkes) for sharing with me their recollections of Fig Tree John; to Jean Corle for her assistance and encouragement; to Kathleen M. Sands for her assistance with the Apache enthnographic materials; to Fran and Marion for help; and to Anne for everything. Grateful acknowledgment is made to the following individuals and organizations for permission to reproduce photographs and to reprint materials: to Louisa Aguilar, Harry C. James, *Desert Magazine,* Nevada C. Colley, and Field

[xiii]

Studios for photographs; to Jean Corle, Lawrence Clark
Powell, and the Department of Special Collections, Research
Library, University of California at Los Angeles, for the
February 18, 1953, letter from Edwin Corle to Lawrence
Clark Powell; to the *Historical Society of Southern Califor-
nia Quarterly* for the passages from the Ulysses S. Grant IV
article; to *Palm Springs Life* for the passage from the
H. E. Marshall article and the photograph from *Palm
Springs Villager;* to Nina Paul Shumway and Leland Yost
for their article from *Desert Magazine*.

INTRODUCTION

FIG TREE JOHN was an American Indian who underwent two major transformations. He was fully aware of the first: his transformation from a traditional Indian living the old way of life in the parched desert to a more modern Indian living the new way of life as a member of a minority group in an irrigated desert surrounded by land-hungry white farmers. The second he never knew about because it took place after his death: his transformation from the highly adaptive Cahuilla Indian he was in real life to the primitive and highly unadaptive Apache Indian he became in the pages of a novel by Edwin Corle.

Fig Tree John lived most of his life in the Colorado Desert of southern California. When he died a very old man in 1927, he had long been known to local residents of the area as a colorful and enigmatic figure who lived down near the Salton Sea, somewhat removed from other Indians and surrounded by white neighbors. Many early travelers, ethnologists, prospectors, tourists, and settlers stopped at his camp to chat with him or to get water from his spring. Several found the old man interesting enough to mention in magazine articles and books about their experiences. A couple of incidents led to newspaper articles about him. And because he "made trouble" for some of his white neighbors about land ownership, the clerks at the Bureau of Indian Affairs found that they were keeping a growing file of correspondence about Fig Tree John.

[xv]

Then, in 1933, a young writer named Edwin Corle (pronounced "korl") came to the Coachella Valley and began
asking questions about Fig Tree John. Where did he live?
What tribe was he from? How did he get along with his
neighbors? Did he have a wife? What happened to his son?
Corle was collecting material for a short story about Fig
Tree John. Later this material would be used for a novel
about him. Someone told him that the old man may have
been an Apache from Arizona, so Corle built his novel
around that "fact," even though he probably knew that Fig
Tree John was really a local Cahuilla (pronounced "ca-*wee*-
yah") Indian who had long made his home in the southern
California desert. Corle, after all, was not writing a biography of Fig Tree John; he was writing a novel about him,
and so he relied more on his own creative instincts than on
verifiable facts. Corle did, however, want his novel to have
a ring of authenticity to it, so he used a real geographical
setting, the names of several real people, and a number of
specific and verifiable biographical facts.

Corle also visited the White Mountain Apache country
of Arizona and spent some days at the library of the Southwest Museum in Los Angeles reading about Apaches, about
how they lived, their feelings toward white people, their
legends, and their religious beliefs. What he found out, however, he did not mind altering for his novel. He incorporated whatever authentic ethnographic background materials suited his purpose, altered other materials, and invented
still others. Just as he was not writing a biography of Fig
Tree John, so he was not writing an anthropological account
of Apache lifeways, and so again he gave his creative
instincts priority over the demands for historical complete-
ness or ethnographic reliability.

When Corle's novel *Fig Tree John* was published in
1935, it was well-received by literary critics, and it has been
reissued several times (well over 100,000 copies have been
sold). The reasons for its popularity among both general
readers and literary critics are obvious enough. The novel
has well-developed and convincing characters, an exciting

plot, and a serious theme. Corle was one of the first American novelists who was able to avoid the pitfalls that have crippled so many of those who have tried to deal with Indian characters. Unlike James Fenimore Cooper, Corle does not heavily romanticize his Indians. Unlike Adolf F. Bandelier, he does not mire them in a swamp of ethnographic detail. Unlike Helen Hunt Jackson, he does not use them primarily as examples to illustrate and reinforce a political argument. And unlike countless other writers, Corle took pains to try to find out what real Indians were like before he wrote fiction about them. In the end he found that in the interest of good fiction he had to leave out much of the factual material he had discovered about real Indians and had to invent some new material. In spite of this, *Fig Tree John* has an authentic backbone of reality which has contributed significantly to its continuing popularity.

It is my purpose to examine the facts about Fig Tree John and Apaches to which Corle had access and to compare these facts with the fiction he produced. This comparison gives us an unusually good opportunity to study what happens when a serious novelist works with "authentic" materials. Not only have I uncovered a large amount of factual information about the life of the real Fig Tree John, but I also have discovered the specific ethnographic sources that Corle used for his background information on Apache life. Supplementing these are other materials demonstrating what Corle thought of Apaches and the "Apache problem," as well as a previously unpublished letter in which Corle describes how he wrote the novel. Together these give us a valuable basis for comparing historical facts with the literary fiction that grew out of them.

Fig Tree John, like any other novel, deserves to be read and judged independently as a self-contained work of fiction. It also deserves to be read in a context provided by the unusually large body of background materials out of which it was written. Such a context can be useful in several ways. For one thing, a comparison of the factual information Corle knew with the fictional account he produced enables us to analyze the kinds of changes he made and to speculate on the reasons why he made them. For example, he transformed the real Fig Tree John from an essentially cooperative and peaceful Cahuilla into an independent and aggressive Apache. He made this change for a number of reasons. For one, successful fiction required — at least in 1935 — an exciting plot and dramatic characterization. For another, Corle was writing for an audience which entertained certain views about what Indians were like, and he may have felt that he could appeal most to that audience if he did not stray too far from familiar stereotypes about the nature and character of the American Indian. Surely, however, the most important reason for the change was that Corle wanted to suggest in his novel a serious theme about the necessity for the American Indian to adopt the ways of the white man, and he could make this theme most emphatic if his main character violently — and tragically — rejected the white man's ways.

A comparison of the factual information that Corle's research uncovered with the fictional account he produced also helps us to understand the focus of the novel. By seeing what patterns emerge in the changes Corle made, we can get a better idea of what effects Corle was trying to achieve. For example, the real Fig Tree John had been friendly and gregarious and had lived his life surrounded by a large family and many friends, both Indian and white. In Corle's novel, however, Fig Tree John lives 500 miles from his homeland and fellow tribesmen, has neither white nor Indian friends, and for family has only a son who gradually rejects him. To see this pattern in Corle's changes is to recognize that one of his purposes was to emphasize his fictional character's utter aloneness by isolating him from other human beings. By so doing Corle focused attention on him and on the effects of his fierce rejection of all ways of life but his own. Corle's theme stands out with greater clarity for us if we can see that it resulted from a conscious change in his factual source materials.

It soon becomes clear in a study of this kind that the

task of the writer of fiction differs from that of the social scientist in four important ways, and we must keep these in mind when we analyze and evaluate novels which deal with historical materials. The writer of fiction has two freedoms which the writer of history or anthropology rarely has — the freedom to depict the thoughts and feelings of his subjects, and the freedom to be deductive. The writer of fiction also has two special responsibilities — the responsibility to be plausible and the responsibility to provide convincing motivation for his characters' actions.

The first of the freedoms was mentioned many years ago by A. L. Kroeber, one of the deans of cultural and historical research on the American Indian. In his introduction to *American Indian Life* (Viking, 1925), a collection of short fictional stories written by noted anthropologists about Indians, Kroeber wrote that "the fictional form of presentation . . . has definite merit. It allows a freedom in depicting or suggesting the thoughts and feelings of the Indian, such as is impossible in a formal, scientific report. In fact, it incites to active psychological treatment, else the tale would lag." The novelist, in other words, can (and must) explore realms of human feeling and human psychology, which the historian and the anthropologist must, for the most part, avoid because of the lack of sufficient evidence in these areas. There is also, of course, insufficient "evidence" for the novelist, but the difference is that the novelist has license to create his own evidence, to demonstrate the feelings and the mental workings of characters he has largely invented.

The second freedom which the writer of fiction has is that he can be deductive, while the social scientist must be inductive. The historian or the anthropologist, in other words, is professionally bound to suggest trends, solutions, or meanings only if they grow from his examination of known facts. The novelist, on the other hand, is free to decide first what conclusions he hopes his reader will reach, what the main ideas or themes of his novel will be, and then to set about working up the particular characters and situations which will demonstrate those conclusions and themes. He need not work this way, but he can if he wants to. For a novelist to take advantage of these freedoms to depict feelings and to develop themes, he must create. He must depart from the known and deal with what is not known, or at least not manifest, until his creation takes form.

While the novelist has freedoms that the historian does not have, he also has responsibilities, or obligations, which the historian does not have. The two most important of these are responsibilities to a different kind of reality than that with which the historian customarily deals. First, the novelist must present characters and actions which are plausible. It does not matter that they *really* existed or what *really* happened; it does matter that they appear to a reader as being the kinds of characters that *could* exist and the kinds of events that *could* happen. A novelist who is not believable is wasting his time. The real Fig Tree John wore a long army coat and a tall silk hat when he went out visiting, but Corle makes no mention of such apparel because, among other reasons that will be discussed later, few of his 1935 readers would have believed it to be true. The novelist's allegiance is at least as much to the appearance of factuality as it is to factuality itself. And, of course, it is important to note here that the audience for whom he is trying to make his work seem plausible is usually not the specialist in Indian culture and history, but the average reader.

The novelist's second responsibility is closely related to the first. He must provide convincing human motivation for everything his characters do. It is not enough for him to tell us that someone did something; he must also tell us, or make it quite clear, why he did it. It is not enough for him to tell us that Fig Tree John threatened certain white people with an empty gun; he also must suggest a convincing reason for the action. Was it done out of recklessness? Carelessness? Desperation? Contempt? Derangement? The anthropologist and the historian, of course, try to provide explanations for human actions, but if they cannot do so, there the matter rests. The novelist, on the other hand, is bound, if he cannot discover an explanation in his factual material, to invent a convincing one. The reality which the novelist seeks is less a factual reality than a psychological reality.

A consideration of these two freedoms and two responsibilities of a writer suggests that in evaluating a novel about Indians, or any work of fiction based on history, we ought not to demand of the novelist that he be fully accurate or scientifically factual in his treatment of his characters and their lives. The serious novelist ought not to be flagrantly irresponsible by having, say, an Apache warrior paddling up a river in a birchbark canoe on his way to a Sundance ceremony, but within certain broad limits, he should be granted the freedom to create. He deserves no more to be criticized for being "inaccurate" than the anthropologist deserves to be criticized for not having a better plot in a book on Hopi kinship systems. These freedoms and responsibilities also suggest that we ought not to disregard the special kind of insight into the American Indian experience which the responsibly creative novelist can give us. If a novelist can convey a convincing human psychological response, if he can manage to show us what a certain character is feeling, then the novelist has fully justified his writing. It seems to me, for example, that the novelist can convey more poignantly than can the social scientist the response of an individual to intense cultural upheaval. I do not suggest, of course, that the fictional approach is better than the scientific one; I suggest merely that there are some things worth saying about human beings that the novelist is better equipped to say than is the social scientist.

To begin the comparison between the real Fig Tree John and Corle's fictional one, Part One is a biographical sketch of Juanito Razon (pronounced "rah-*sone*"), the real, or historical, Fig Tree John. This section is of importance because it gives us historical information about the life of a specific and ordinary American Indian. Historians and anthropologists frequently write about groups or tribes of Indians — where they lived, who they fought, when they migrated, how they worshipped, and how they live today.

Occasionally an individual Indian is the subject of a study, but until recently these have been almost exclusively important spiritual, military, or political leaders. Rarely do we read studies of an ordinary individual Indian, for rarely, unless the subject is still living, is there enough material available.

Fig Tree John was a minor chieftan or *capitan* of his small village; he lived to a somewhat riper age than most Indians; he was unusual enough to have attracted certain kinds of attention. But he was essentially an ordinary "middle-class" Indian. He earned his living in unspectacular ways, and he had no lasting influence on the important spiritual or political affairs of his people.

Because of the documents available, many of which are reproduced in the following pages, and because of other information available from people who were still living in 1974 and who remembered Fig Tree John, we have a chance for a rare glimpse at the life and character of such a man. Because most of the information we have deals with Fig Tree John during the last 25 years of his life, the glimpse is at best a partial one. We do, however, have an unusual opportunity to look at some of the problems one Indian man had to face in the first quarter of the twentieth century, and at some of the mechanisms for survival which he had to develop in order to maintain his life, his rights, and his dignity in a rapidly changing world.

The biographical materials in Part One provide a basis for instructive comparison with the fictional materials which Corle developed from them. Having made the comparison, we shall be in a position to analyze in Part Two the kinds of changes Corle made in transforming fact into fiction, and to understand to what a great extent the need for memorable character, for strong action, and especially for sustained theme took precedence over the need to be factually complete or historically accurate.

A comparison of the fictional Fig Tree John with his historical counterpart, far from lowering my respect for the novel, vastly increases it, and vastly increases my admiration for Corle's skill as a novelist. It is clear that Corle altered what he knew to be the historical truth about his character for a number of clearly defined purposes. One of these purposes, as we have already seen, was to advance his theme about the necessity for the American Indian to assimilate the ways of the white man. To show as emphatically as possible the bad effects of nonassimilation, Corle made his fictional Fig Tree John far more isolated, far more belligerent, and far more resistant to change than the real Fig Tree John had been. Corle then contrasted his character with the far more genial and malleable character of Fig Tree John's son, Johnny Mack, who does eventually assimilate the white man's ways.

Although I do not personally endorse all of the political and social implications of Corle's theme, I am nevertheless impressed with how fully he maintains artistic control over his materials. If his historical materials did not permit him to say what he wanted to say, Corle felt no qualms about departing from them and inventing additional materials in order to establish a character and a set of circumstances which would do for him what the factual truth could not have done.

In Part Two I also deal with the implications of the fact that Corle made his character an Apache immigrant from Arizona rather than a Cahuilla Indian who was native to southern California. The ethnographic background which Corle provided in his novel, then, is Apache material, much of which Corle learned about by reading a 1930 anthropological monograph on the Fort Apache (White Mountain) Indians of Arizona. Here again we have a basis for comparison, for we can look both at the ethnographic material which Corle worked from, and at the use Corle made of it in his novel. Again we find that from this source Corle used only what would help his novel. Other Apache ethnographic material that we find in *Fig Tree John* was either adapted by Corle from other factual sources or was invented by him. He wanted to make his materials serve him by using them to provide his novel with a core of authenticity, with a fixed cultural orientation from which to measure cultural change (or the lack of it), and with an implicit explanation for certain of his main character's opinions and actions.

Corle's *Fig Tree John,* then, although it grew out of biographical and ethnographic facts, is not biographically reliable or ethnographically complete. It is, however, a good novel. Corle was very much in control of his materials, and it is fortunate, from a literary standpoint, that he always gave the artistic and thematic integrity of his work a higher priority than he gave its historical accuracy.

FIG TREE JOHN

IN FACT

AN INDEPENDENT CAHUILLA

AN INDEPENDENT CAHUILLA

In January of 1900 a wagon drawn by two horses made its way west across the Colorado Desert in southern California. In it was a woman named Frances Anthony. With a couple of friends she was out on a two-week sightseeing trip through the desert. Frances Anthony later wrote up what was to become the first published account of a visit to Fig Tree John's home. She described the alkaline soil and the desert bushes which she saw as she descended into the Salton Sink, that enormous dried-up basin which centuries before had been filled with salt water and had possibly been connected with the Gulf of California. Now the basin was entirely dry, but she described the evidence of an old shore line on the mountains surrounding the basin: the clear color demarcations on the rocks, the pebbly "beaches" on the gentler slopes at what would have been sea level long ago. She described the buildings, derricks, and railroad cars that were part of the salt-mining operation near the very bottom of the dry basin — some 275 feet below sea level. Her destination was the home of Fig Tree John, where she hoped to find lodging for the night. After asking a passing Indian which road to take, she and her friends set out:

When we had gone what seemed far enough we could see no sign of a settlement, and should have thought that we were going into a wilderness; but just then we perceived a faint smoke rising straight ahead. Soon we made out the yellow leaves of a

[3]

cottonwood tree — then the green of a palm tree, and soon, under the smoke, the tule-thatched roof of the house. There were several buildings of brush with tule roofs. Their color is so much like that of the soil and the general brown of most vegetation during the winter that one might even be looking and pass them by but for a smoke or the movement of an animal to call closer attention.

Fig Tree John himself met us at the gate. He assigned us one of his brush houses, brought us an arm-load of the finest dry mesquite wood, showed us how to make the fire in the middle of the one room, and pointed out the manner in which the smoke rose to the ridge pole and then went out at the open end. Through it all his manner was as hospitable as any white man's could be. Our house was built without boards or nails; and, though open at the east end and without a floor, was a good shelter from the wind even in those first days of January.

At the four corners and in the middle of each end posts were set in the ground. The tops were forked, and in the forks were laid the plates and ridgepole. The sides and end were filled in with straight desert brush, the roof thatched with tules and all fastened with strips of rawhide and palm leaves.

Fig Tree John is known by that name because he is the distinguished owner of an orchard of fig trees. His Spanish name is Juan Razon, but his Indian name is a secret. In the evening he, with his wife and baby, visited us, and next morning he breakfasted with us.[1]

The "real" name of this hospitable desert fig grower and motel keeper was Juanito Razon. He was variously referred to also as Juan, Juaneta, and Juanita Razon. He is said himself to have insisted on the feminine *-a* ending rather than the masculine *-o*, and on placing an accent on the final vowel in his last name (*Razón*),[2] but since he was carried on the tribal roll and was known to most writers as Juanito Razon, he shall be referred to as such here. The name "Fig Tree John" was a white man's name for him, derived from his ownership of a productive orchard of fig trees. By the end of his life many of his Indian friends knew him and called him by this name, but it was always really a nickname. Frances Anthony reported that "his Indian name is a secret"; if he had such a name, then it is still a secret, for his official name for himself was always the Spanish form.

TRIBAL AFFILIATION

Juanito Razon was a Cahuilla Indian, a member of a small Mission tribe native to southern California. The "Fig Tree John" of Edwin Corle's novel is a White Mountain Apache from Arizona who comes to the Salton Sea in 1906 with his favorite wife and stays on until his death in 1928. Edwin Corle, however, did not invent the idea that Fig Tree John was an Apache. He was told by Edward P. Carr, who had been Juanito Razon's neighbor, that he was "certain that Fig Tree was an Apache."[3] A man named Jim Black once thought that Juanito Razon looked like an Apache and spoke a few words to him in the Apache language. The old man responded in the same tongue and apparently "admitted he came from Arizona many years before."[4] It may be that the cause of such misinformation was Juanito Razon's physical stature. He was unusually short for a Cahuilla — around 5'2" tall according to Louisa Aguilar, a surviving daughter of one of Juanito Razon's nephews. Perhaps it was that the land he claimed as his own was further south than the land where most of the other Cahuillas lived, so that he appeared to be isolated from others of his tribe. Perhaps it was simply that Juanito Razon somewhat resembled the feared Geronimo, photographs of whom were legion.

Edward H. Davis, the amateur ethnologist and collector of Indian materials of all kinds, saw the old man at an Indian funeral in 1917 and thought he looked like an Apache. He wrote in his notebooks, only recently edited and published, that "I studied his dark, seamed, old face, and tried to locate a resemblance to someone I had seen before. His face was free of hair and deeply wrinkled, small nose slightly Roman, lips a thin, straight line, eyes deep-set and beady; chin square and in profile straight down from the lower lip; hair only slightly gray. He was active; his expression was crafty and one knew instinctively that if he bore a grudge, he would be absolutely merciless and cruel in revenge. Then I realized he bore a resemblance to the cruelest chief of the *Apaches,*

Geronimo."[5] Perhaps he had learned a few words of the Apache language from some wandering Arizona Indians and so confused some people as to his origins.

My own theory is that Juanito Razon may well have wanted to let his white neighbors *think* he was an Apache. He was discovered to be something of a bluffer when he wielded an apparently unusable rifle against trespassers. Perhaps, in the struggle to defend what he believed to be his rights, he found he could command more respect if he were thought to be a tough and dangerous Apache rather than just another "friendly" Cahuilla. The Cahuillas had long lived in the deserts, hills, and mountains of southern California gathering mesquite beans, acorns, and piñon nuts, and hunting various animals such as rabbits, deer, sheep, quail, and wood rats. They never waged war on the white people who moved in to settle on their lands; they sought instead to make treaties. In view of the fact that Juanito Razon had trouble asserting his claim to the lands he lived on, it might well have been a decided advantage to him to let his neighbors — especially the close ones like Edward P. Carr — believe, if they wanted to, that he was an Apache, for the Apaches were famous for firmly resisting any invasions of their territory.

Whatever the reasons for the idea among some white men that he was an Apache, it is clear that Juanito Razon was a local Cahuilla. He was listed in the tribal roll as a Cahuilla, and his father was listed as "Chief Razon," possibly the Cahuilla chieftain whose name appears as one of the signers of the Treaty of Temecula in 1852. He told a white visitor to his camp around 1917 that he was born, not to the east in Arizona, but at Coyote Mountain, some 20 miles to the west.[6] His Cahuilla lineage and clan affiliation are discussed by early ethnologists.[7] Juanito Razon was a leader, or *capitan,* of local Cahuillas, and he was active in Cahuilla ceremonies. Cahuillas seem not to have questioned his right to claim to be one of them. I suppose it is possible that one of his parents or grandparents may have been an Apache, but it seems highly unlikely that as an

Apache immigrant Juanito Razon could have fooled a group of Cahuillas into thinking he was one of them.

Another misconception among many whites about Juanito Razon is that he was somehow isolated from his people. Perhaps this notion derives from the theory that he was an Apache, and, therefore, cut off from his own tribe. Perhaps, again, it was his apparent physical isolation; his clan had always been one of the southernmost Cahuilla clans, and his refusal to leave his ancestral territory when the whites moved in caused him to appear to be cut off from other Indians. It is quite probable that there were members of his own tribe he did not like, and no doubt there were some of his tribe who did not like him, but to say that he was some kind of an outcast or hermit is simply not true. There are reports that Juanito Razon once set up a line of posts on what he considered to be his north boundary line and "forbade even those of his own race to cross it";[8] that, because he refused to submit to the white man as the rest of the Cahuillas had, he had "turned against his own people";[9] that he "withdrew himself even from his own tribal brethren";[10] that he "preferred to live as a hermit remote from his own people and civilization."[11] There seems to be no basis for such suggestions.

Juanito Razon was isolated only in that his home — the land where his people had always lived — was off the reservation and somewhat removed from the main Cahuilla villages. He was a loner only in that he refused to move. But Indians were welcome at his spring, and he made frequent trips to visit his friends and family elsewhere. Louisa Aguilar, in a 1974 interview, said that Juanito Razon frequently traveled as far as Banning on the train to visit Henry Matthews, her father and his nephew. Jane Penn, Director of the Malki Museum near Banning, California, and part Cahuilla herself, insisted that Juanito Razon neither withdrew himself from his tribe nor was cast out or shunned by the tribe. She thought he was different from other Cahuillas only in that he wore distinctive clothes and was more than usually resistant to white encroachments on his property.

He participated in Cahuilla rituals even though, like many Cahuillas, he had become a Christian. Dr. Lowell Bean, an anthropologist who has done extensive work among the Cahuillas, wrote that "many Cahuillas I have worked with remember him well. He was both a picturesque figure and a venerated man. He was a man of knowledge and respected by all. He was an active participant in Cahuilla rituals."[12]

As for those posts which Juanito Razon was said to have set up on his property line, there is a probable explanation in a rather unlikely source, the United States Senate Executive Documents for 1892. The affair which concerned the United States Senate had begun a couple of years earlier when Horatio N. Rust, Indian agent for several of the small Mission tribes in southern California, refused to commission an Indian named Will Pablo as "captain" of the Potrero Indians (a group which lived to the north and west of the Cahuillas). Rust refused to make the commission on the grounds that Pablo was a drunkard, that he did not have a regular job, and that he did not adequately support his wife and child. Besides, Rust preferred to deal directly with his Indian charges and did not feel that he could profitably work through native representatives or local captains. Rust's refusal to recognize Will Pablo as captain infuriated him, and Pablo began a systematic program of activities designed to undermine the authority of Rust. Pablo went to a lawyer named John Brown, who urged him to send a petition to Washington asking for Rust's removal as Indian agent. Pablo got some 200 Indians to sign the petition. Later, by urging the Indians to take their children out of the government school and to send them to the Catholic school some miles away, Pablo virtually emptied the government school at Potrero. He told the Indians that a "Messiah" was coming to destroy all of the white men. (Almost certainly, this was a belated reference to the Nevada Paiute Wovoka's Ghost Dance teachings of the late 1890s.) Pablo even made contact with the public press and told some newspaper reporters how Rust had leased his land out to white ranchers without reimbursing him, and how Rust had subverted the will of the Indians by deposing old Chief Cabazon and appointing his own choice as tribal chief. It was the news-paper reports, which appeared in major newspapers as far away as San Francisco and St. Louis, which eventually brought the whole matter to the attention of the United States Senate, and as a result of a Senate investigation, a number of letters have been preserved in the public record.

One of these letters helps to explain what Juanito Razon's neighbors interpreted as "isolationist" behavior when the old man set up fence posts and refused to let other Indians come beyond them. One of Will Pablo's schemes for under-mining Agent Rust's authority was to join forces with the deposed Chief Cabazon and to travel from village to village appointing Indian captains. This set up a political organi-zation to rival the influence of the agent among the various tribes. In a letter of May 13, 1892, Rust wrote to the Com-missioner of Indian Affairs in Washington, D.C., to ask for permission to build a jail so that he could imprison Cabazon and Pablo. As part of his justification for the request, he complained that "Pablo conspires with Cabazon . . . and travels from village to village saying I am deposed, or that he will do it. . . . He promises them much and keeps them constantly uneasy. He has issued some twenty commissions to 'his captains,' who are pleased to do his bidding if con-trary to my wishes. They have plowed and closed old roads long used by the public, and he allots lands and locates his friends in a most unreasonable manner. By his lieutenants he directs in many little ways matters which constantly cause irritation and uneasiness. Now comes a complaint that his captain forbids another Indian to cross an unoccupied field when he needs to go to harvest his crop, said captain having set his fence posts in the old road."[13]

It seems clear that Juanito Razon was one of Cabazon's (and Pablo's) twenty "captains," because 25 years later, around 1917, he showed an "aged document" to a white visitor at his camp. The document showed that Cabazon formally appointed Juanito Razon to be *capitan* of the Agua Dulce Tuba village and gave him authority over the lands from the Hiawat ridge of the Santa Rosa Mountains to Black Rabbit Peak.[14]

Rust does not give the name of the village captain who set the posts in the road. Indeed, Pablo may have delivered general instructions from Chief Cabazon to a number of the village captains to carry out such activities. Rust's letter, however, suggests to us that Juanito Razon's action was part of a larger plan to identify village boundaries, to consolidate the power of one of the Cahuilla factions, and to offer resistance to an autocratic and possibly dishonest Indian agent. The posts suggest, then, not that Juanito Razon was somehow anti-Indian or a loner, but that he was pro-Indian in his activities and was very much involved in Cahuilla affairs. His placing of the posts, indeed, may have been designed to keep certain Indians off land he was appointed to protect for members of his own clan or faction, but surely it is inaccurate to conclude that it was meant to keep all Cahuillas away.

Juanito Razon's pride in his people, his knowledge of their history and lore, and his willingness to share his camp with them are illustrated by several accounts. Frances Anthony, who had visited his camp in 1900, heard him describe the sudden flood that had once roared into the valley and carried off many of his people: "Yes! Yes! in one night came much water and killed many Indians, many Indians!"[15] Louisa Aguilar remembered distinctly that her father, Henry Matthews, the half-white nephew of Juanito Razon, had been much impressed with how much Juanito Razon knew about old Indian trails, markers, and markings in the area. Her father had learned a great deal from Juanito Razon, one of the last real experts in Cahuilla lore and survival in the desert and mountains.

Nevada C. Colley, writing of the experiences of Charley Brown, her husband's uncle and one of the first white settlers in Juanito Razon's part of the desert, tells of the time the old man had shown Brown some huge stone structures, apparently fish traps, high up on the shoreline of the ancient sea which had centuries before filled the Salton Basin: "Fig Tree stood erect and studied the work of his forefathers with pride; he spoke slowly . . . 'Maybe one-hundred, maybe

two-hundred years ago, my people lived in mountains. . . .
My people built these fish traps.' " Colley also tells of the
time Charley Brown visited Juanito Razon's camp in 1918
and saw "a number of children" running about, as well as
four women.[16] At the camp of a hermit or tribal exile we
would scarcely expect to find so many Indians, or so much
pride in and knowledge of their ways. The notion, then, that
Juanito Razon held himself above other local Cahuillas, or
that they somehow rejected him, seems to have been a peculi-
arly white notion, not an Indian one.

HOMELAND

Far from being a "Johnny-come-lately" to Cahuilla territory, Juanito Razon appears to have spent most of his life
near what is now the Salton Sea. Frances Anthony had visited his camp on the west side of the Salton Sink in 1900,
but gave no indication of how long her host had lived there.
Another visitor to the camp five years later unwittingly gives
us a clue. Jocie Wallace, apparently a Catholic missionary,
described for readers of a Roman Catholic publication how
the desert Indians lived, then went on to describe her visit
to Juanito Razon's camp and her experience with one of his
sons:

Most of the Indians can talk English, and some read well.
They are honest and agreeable, and the most of them are Catho-
lics. They are becoming more and more like the white man in their
habits of eating; they use dried and canned fruit, also fresh fruits
in warm weather, but more heat-producing foods in winter. They
use much soap, and keep their clothes very respectable. Their
houses are made by skillfully working arrow weed into a frame of
timber and wire, which is so tight that they will turn water and
keep out dust, and indeed they trim off the rough edges so neatly
and nicely that they look quite homelike. Their houses are always
built beneath some large shade trees, as cottonwood, willow,
palms, or pala verde, and then they are sure to be near water.
They spend most of their time out in the shade of their yard trees.
One old Indian chief known as Fig Tree John got his name
from the large old fig-trees which he has. Thirty of his trees are at
least thirty years old, then he has quite an orchard of younger

ones. He says he once found a little wild tree and got a start from its cuttings; however, his trees are now of the finest and earliest bearing of the country. The figs are about the size and shape of a turkey egg, and delicious in flavor, being very sweet. They ripen the first of May and his son ships them to the Los Angeles market at twenty-five cents a pound. The picture is of Fig Tree John, his wife, and two of his grandchildren. Indians do not like to have their pictures taken, but as we visited them, gave them some oranges, admired the fig-trees and baskets, we gained the old man's good graces. Still when he heard the word pictures he began to move toward his cabin, but on the offer of money he soon made ready, and having the dollar safely in his own hand, he stood up for the picture.

One of Fig Tree John's sons spent five years in the Kansas and Arizona school, and he seems quite intelligent. After he had read several copies of the YOUTH'S INSTRUCTOR, *Signs,* and *Life Boat,* he told me that he loved to study the good things in my papers, and if I did not care, he would like to rent or borrow my Bible, as his had been stolen from him by another Indian. I put him off, and began to plan and pray to see what I should do, and at last I decided to give up my cherished treasure, which was the first Bible I ever called my own, having worked hard when but a child to earn it as a premium. I gave it to him the next time he came, and the many "Thank you's" and happy smiles more than paid me for the Bible, as I have a new one. Since then he told me that it taught him to be good, and he loved it very much.[17]

Because Jocie Wallace says that Juanito Razon had 30 fig trees, which were "at least thirty years old," and that he had started them himself from the cuttings of another tree, we can assume that he had lived near the Salton area at least since 1875. That date is corroborated by an early ethnological report that Juanito Razon's clan, the *wantciñakik tamiana-witcem* clan, had moved with him sometime around 1870 from its old location at Fish Springs a couple of miles to the south.[18]

Whatever the exact date of his arrival, Juanito Razon could not have stayed at what had come to be called "Fig Tree John Spring" much longer than 1905. In February of that year the Colorado River went on its famous rampage. High flood waters tore through the control gates designed to release measured amounts of river water into the recently built irrigation canal. To their amazement and dismay the engineers found, after the flood waters had subsided, that the full flow of the Colorado River had been diverted. Instead of flowing straight south through Mexico to the Gulf of California, the river had completely changed channels

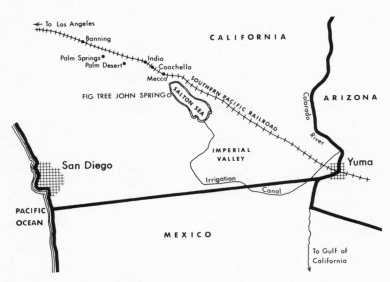

A map of the southern California desert regions showing Juanito Razon's homeland. In 1905 the flooding Colorado River changed course and rushed down the irrigation canal into the dry basin known as the Salton Sink. During the next two years the river slowly formed the 45-mile-long Salton Sea and drove Juanito Razon out of his home at the original fig orchard.

and was rushing west through the irrigation canal to the Imperial Valley, the fertile, flat land, south of the Salton Sink, which the canal had been meant to irrigate. The river soon completed its own channel into the dry below-sea-level desert basin, and the basin, lacking any outlet, began to fill up. It was two years before the engineers could successfully divert the river back into its old channel and control once again the flow of water down the canal, but in that interval the dry Salton Sink became a very wet Salton Sea, some 45 miles long and nearly 20 miles wide. The rising flood waters

had gradually inundated Juanito Razon's fig orchard and
home, and the old man and his family had been forced to
move to higher ground.

In October of 1906 an article appeared in a San Bernardino, California, newspaper, which in part bears directly
on Juanito Razon's situation. The article is quoted in full
because of the attitudes about Indians which it reveals:

INDIAN AGENT SAYS RAZON DREAMED

Red Man is Enjoying Life in Salton Basin

L. A. Wright, of San Jacinto, U.S. Indian Agent for Southern
California, was in the city yesterday, having been out at the San
Manuel reservation, north of Patton, looking after the government's charges there, and supplying a number of aged and sick
Indians with rations, which is done regularly, there being quite
a number of that class who are unable to work. All able bodied
Indians who can secure employment are compelled to work, and
these are not supplied with rations, except under extraordinary
circumstances.

Indian agent Wright takes exceptions to the reports circulated
by Captain Juaneta Razon, from the Torres reservation, in the
vicinity of the Salton sea, to the effect that large numbers of the
red skins in that section have lost their homes from the ever rising
flood, which reports have been given wide circulation by getting
into the newspapers.

Razon's Dream

Mr. Wright states the facts are that the only Indians to lose
their homes from this cause were Razon, who is better known as
"Fig Tree John," and his brother, whose ranches adjoined and
were located on lands recently inundated, at the south end [*sic,
Razon lived on the west side*] of the sea. The three principal villages in the Torres reservation, which lies to the west of the sea,
are Torres, Martinez, where the government school is located,
and Alimo Benita, and none of these villages are much closer than
10 miles to the present lines of the sea.

As to the report that the Indians are now in a much worse
condition than when they became government charges, Agent
Wright draws a startling comparison. He says that then they were
roaming about the desert, existing on mesquite beans and jack

rabbits, living a nomadic life, next door to starvation all the time. Now most of them have good ranches, on which they grow good crops of alfalfa, melons and other produce, besides raising considerable live stock. And many of them have good comfortable homes and are quite prosperous farmers. As for showing how they are getting into agricultural pursuits, the agent pointed out that the first shipment of cantaloupes from that section this season was made by an Indian, Martin Lopez, in Alimo Benita village, the shipment consisting of two crates, 16 melons each, and they netting him $32. or $1. each.

As to the case of Captain Razon, or "Fig Tree John," as he is known to the residents of the desert, he can at once take up new lands anywhere in the reservation or near the villages and establish a new home just as good as the former one, if he wishes.[19]

Whether he wished to or not, Juanita Razon had to "take up new lands" and "establish a new home." As nearly as can be determined from such maps and information as are available, Juanito Razon's spring would have been under at least five feet of water at the height of the flood in March of 1907. The old man packed his belongings and moved a few miles northeast to higher ground at the Agua Dulce Spring. Evaporation eventually reduced the sea to its present level some 20 feet below the high-water mark of March 1907. Juanito Razon could have moved back to his former spring, but by then his first orchard was mostly destroyed and new trees were taking hold at his new place at Agua Dulce Spring. Though he never gave up his claim to the lands at the old spring, he stayed on at Agua Dulce until April 11, 1927 when he died from influenza. He was buried in the Catholic cemetery on the reservation.

AGE

How old was Juanito Razon at his death in 1927? There have been considerable differences of opinion on this question. The tribal roll listed his year of birth as 1839, which would have made him 88 at his death. Edward H. Davis wrote in his notebook after he attended a funeral on the reservation in 1917: "On one side of me was Fig-Tree John, who had come with his wife to join in the ceremony. He was ninety years old."[20] If that were true, then Juanito Razon would have been born in 1827 and would have been an even 100 years old at his death. A man who visited his camp in 1913 reported that the Indian "was said to be ninety-one years old."[21] If that were the correct age in 1913, Juanito Razon would have been born in 1822 and would have been 105 when he died. Johnny Mack Razon, on the other hand, said that his father was 135 when he died.[22]

It seems unlikely that even Juanito Razon himself knew when he was born, because there were no birth records for Indians in those days. Jane Penn, director of the Malki Museum, related that even today many of the very old Indians do not know exactly how old they are. If asked when they were born, they may remember a parent's telling them something about how it was "when the yucca were in bloom," but of course that would indicate only the season of the year, not the year itself. Neither she nor Louisa Aguilar, a surviving relative, claimed to know Juanito Razon's age at death, although both said that he was very old and very wrinkled in his last years. While we can never be sure, then, exactly how old Juanito Razon was when he died, we can narrow the limits a little from the nearly 50-year range of estimates that have been made.

It seems quite clear that the estimate of 135 years is considerably inflated. According to the *Guinness Book of World Records,* which states that the oldest *authenticated* age for a human being is 113, inflated claims are not uncommon: "No single subject is more obscured by vanity, deceit, falsehood, and deliberate fraud than the extremes of human longevity. Extreme claims are generally made on behalf of the aged rather than by them."[23] If Johnny Mack Razon had been right his father would have exceeded the world's record by 22 years. While this is not impossible, it seems unlikely in view of the other estimates which have been made. Another problem with the age of 135 is that, since Johnny Mack Razon was born in 1875 (according to the agency "Marriage Card" for Juanito Razon), if he had been right about the old man's age, his father would have been well over 80 when he sired Johnny. This is not impossible, but, again, it seems unlikely.

5—153 a.

MARRIAGE CARD.

First .... Marriage. Sex Male .... Census or Allotment No. 90-1920
(1st, 2d, 3d, etc.)

Name ...... Razon, Juanito, ... Tribe Martinez (Cahuilla) Mission

Married .... 1861 .... How Tribal Custom.
(By tribal custom, or legally.)

Married to whom Razon, Matilda, ... Census or Allotment No. 91-1920

If divorced, When .... Where ....
(Date.) (Place.)

If divorced, How ....
(By tribal custom, or legally.)

CHILDREN BORN OF THIS MARRIAGE.

CENSUS OR ALLOTMENT No.	SEX	NAME	BORN	DIED
	F	Roxey, Savilia Razon,	1870	
93-1920	M	Razon, John Mack.	1875	
96-1920	M	Razon, Jake. *not a son*	1877	
92-1920	M	Razon, Lario, *(but nephew)*	1890	

See Marriage Cards Nos. .... and .... for half brothers and half sisters of these children.

Bureau of Indian Affairs

This "Marriage Card" is still on file at the Bureau of Indian Affairs Agency
in Riverside, California. It shows Juanito Razon's marriage date, as well as
the birth dates of his three surviving children and a nephew. His "Individual
History Card" (also on file at the Agency but not reproduced here) gives
1839 as the year of Juanito Razon's own birth, but that was probably only a
guess. No birth certificate or verifiable record of his birth date is available.

The agency records show that Juanito Razon was born in 1839, but, in view of the absence of any birth certificate, this was probably only a guess on the part of the man who wrote it down. This date is consistent with other records in the agency files (then Juanito Razon would have been 22 when he married in 1861, and 31 when his first child was born in 1870), but not even the agency officials seem to have taken the date seriously. An exchange of letters in 1923 between a Mr. O. J. Mitchell, of Los Angeles, and Superintendent Charles L. Ellis, who was in charge of the Indian agency in Riverside, California, shows how uncertain the officials were. Mitchell wrote to Ellis four years before the old man's death: [24]

O. J. Mitchell to Superintendent Ellis, October 9, 1923

Dear Sir:

Through the courtesy and kindness of Postmaster Lykken, Palm Spring, I am given your address.

The object of this communication is to obtain, if practicable, a little biographic history of Figtree John, who lives about forty miles east of Palm Springs at Salton Sea. I should also like to have one of his latest photographs. This quest is in behalf of Dr. St. Louis Estes, of Chicago. Doctor Estes is a great believer and advocate of the eating of raw foods, dairy products, and vegetables, and lectures and publishes a monthly magazine along these lines. Recently, I met one Andrew Moro, Mission Indian, at the University Club, here. During our talk, he advised me of Figtree, particularly commenting on his great age of 130 years, and also on his system of living and eating of raw foods and vegetables, and staying in the open. As this is a subject that appeals especially to Doctor Estes, I immediately wrote him, inquiring if he would like an article about Figtree, as his age is so much along the line of his health and life talks, that a man, by right and clean living and proper eating, should easily live to 150 years. As I suspected, Doctor Estes, in response to my letter, wrote that he would be very much interested in having the purposed article about Figtree, together with a copy of his latest picture, and would like to run it in the November issue of his magazine, "Back To Nature." On the strength of this, I made a trip to Riverside, Sunday, September 23, to find Figtree; but, on arriving there, I disappointingly found that he lived at the other end of Riverside County, not at Riverside, as I had been previously informed. As it is impracticable for me to make a trip to Salton Sea, I am resorting to the mails for the carrying-out of this mission for Doctor Estes. In having your address, I am anticipating that, if consistent, you may be able to tell me all I desire to know, and also furnish the desired picture of Figtree, at my expense of course. Moro also told me there were two or three other very old Indians living with Figtree, one of them being 138. Perhaps the history of these, too, would help in the writing of the Figtree article. I shall be glad to send you a copy of "Back To Nature," if you are interested, either for yourself or your family (if you are married).

Superintendent Ellis's reply is remarkable for its patient helpfulness in response to what must have seemed to be something of a crackpot letter:

Superintendent Ellis to O. J. Mitchell, October 23, 1923

Dear Sir:

I regret the delay in answering your letter of October 9th, but I have been in the field for nearly two weeks and have but just returned.

I have no photograph of Fig Tree John (Juanito Razon is the real name) and as I do not expect to return to the desert for some time I cannot promise definitely that I can obtain one.

Fig Tree John is quite a noted character, and while there is no accurate record concerning his age it appears probable that he is well over 100 years of age. He is well preserved, and does not look to be 100. He was unquestionably born before the American occupation of California (1844–7) and as the records prior to that time were in Mexican hands they have either been lost or destroyed and no one can say with any degree of accuracy his exact age. A Riverside man states that Fig Tree John told him that he remembered when he (John) was a young man of Spanish (probably Mexican) soldiers going through the valley to San Gabriel Mission. As the Missions in California passed to the control of the State under the secularization act in 1832 it will readily appear that John's age is at least 100.

Like most of the Indians, Fig Tree has spent most of his life in the open, usually moving to the mountains in the summer and to the desert in the winter. Lately he has been spending most of his time in the desert regions.

John may be eating raw foods and vegetables, but his diet is not confined to such. The Government gives him a monthly allowance or credit at a store near his abode, and a check of the bills indicates that he purchases and uses such articles as flour, beans, rice, dry salt pork, bacon, etc.

The vague and inconclusive reference to Spanish soldiers is, of course, not proof of anything. Nor is Juanito Razon's own claim that he was 97 in 1917,[25] an age which would have made him 107 at his death ten years later. It might well have been to his advantage in requesting food rations or in establishing claim to certain lands to say that he was older than he really was.

We shall never know Juanito Razon's exact age but, all things considered, it is probably safe to assume that he was nearly 100 at the time of his death. Whatever the exact figure, Juanito Razon was an old man, and the history of recorded knowledge about him is almost entirely the history of the white man's contact with an old Indian. Juanito Razon may well have been one of the friendly Cahuilla Indians encountered in this area by Lieutenant Parke during the expedition in 1853 to survey the desert for the best route for the Southern Pacific Railroad.[26] Almost certainly Juanito Razon had dealings with United States soldiers in this early period. In general, however, recorded contact with him does not begin until the turn of the century, shortly before the rising sea forced him to move to the Agua Dulce Spring. By then he was well into his 60s, at the least.

For all we know, then, to write the history of Juanito Razon using the materials we have available to us may be a little like writing a biography of Dwight Eisenhower after he left Washington and moved to Gettysburg. We may be missing most of the excitement. Certainly we are getting only a partial picture of the man's life.

FAMILY

Actually, of course, a partial picture is all we can get even of Juanito Razon's last quarter-century. Such contact as is recorded is not only spotty but, as we have seen, often confused and inaccurate. For further examples, let us consider what several visitors had to say about the old man's family. Frances Anthony, who spent the night at his camp in 1900, records seeing Juanito Razon "with his wife and baby."[27] Ulysses S. Grant, IV, visited in 1913 and reported finding him "with his squaw and two young boys." The woman looked to be younger than Juanito Razon, and "could have been the mother of the two young boys, who

Desert Magazine

*Juanito and Matilda Razon in their buckboard,
which was said to have had very squeaky axles.*

appeared to be around nine years old." Grant, however, wonders who the father may have been: "precisely who sired these youngsters, considering John's advance[d] age, may have been a family secret we felt was better left unexplored."[28] Grant apparently found it easier to suspect a cuckolding than to wonder whether those children could have been his grandchildren, his nephews, or even just his friends.

Actually, they were probably his grandchildren. In 1900 Juanito Razon's oldest child would have been 30 years old; in 1913 the oldest child would have been 43.

When Jocie Wallace visited Juanito Razon in 1905, she took a picture of Razon with his wife and "two of his grand-children."[29] No doubt the older was the one Frances Anthony had thought to be the old man's baby. Perhaps the younger was one of those who Grant later thought were the old man's nine-year-old sons. Juanito Razon might well have been called upon to raise or take in his grandchildren. Jane Penn reported that Johnny Mack Razon's wife had died when she was quite young, leaving him with a daughter, Minnie, to take care of; perhaps Juanito Razon and his wife were called upon to help raise their granddaughter. Louisa Aguilar reminded me that "the Indian way" is to open one's home to guests, especially to relatives. White visitors, unfamiliar with the "extended family" and hospi-tality traditions of Indians, seem to have generally assumed that any children around the old man's home were his own. This sort of misapprehension no doubt led some observers to think that he had had three or four wives.[30]

To set the record straight about Juanito Razon's family connections, he was the son of "Chief Razon" and "Suella Razon," the latter raised at San Gabriel, California. He had several brothers and sisters. (One sister, Louisa, married Thomas Matthews, a white Mormon, and one of their sons, Henry, married a Cahuilla woman and had seven children, among them Louisa Aguilar.) In 1861 Juanito Razon mar-ried Matilda by tribal custom. A daughter, Savilia, was born in 1870. Of their surviving sons, Johnny Mack was born in 1875, and Jake in 1877. One of these sons, it is not clear which, apparently "spent five years in the Kansas and Ari-zona school."[31] When Juanito Razon died in 1927 only Savilia, Johnny Mack, and Jake survived him. Matilda had died some years earlier, on March 6, 1923, at an age of 80 or more.

CLOTHING

The one thing which virtually everyone who saw Juanito Razon in his last quarter-century noticed about him was his clothing. His favorite outfit consisted of a black silk top hat and an army coat with brass buttons. These he wore when he went out to church, to town, to ceremonials, to celebrations, or to have his picture taken. Many photographs of the old man show him in this rather bizarre costume. Why did he wear these clothes? Surprisingly few have speculated on this. Perhaps he wore them to make himself a more desirable subject for paying photographers. Perhaps the unusual clothes were a mark of distinction or special status among his acquaintances. Perhaps the top hat was a kind of compensation for his shortness, or even for the shape of his head (Louisa Aguilar told me that some Indians nicknamed him "bullet-head"). Perhaps the coat was meant to impress people with his military background and capability. Perhaps he just thought he looked good in this outfit, or felt comfortable in it. Whatever the reason, he was proud of his costume and considered it a kind of personal trademark. This outfit was so much associated with his personality that, when he died, he was buried in it.

Many have wondered where the old man got the uniform. Johnny Mack, who admitted that he really did not know, thought that perhaps his father had picked it up when he was in Los Angeles at "some kind of Indian meeting."[32] Juanito Razon himself, in 1910, told his white neighbor, Charley Brown, that he had gotten it as payment for helping some thirsty soldiers lost in the desert: "Big general chasing Mexicans, got lost in desert. I give water, tell which way to go. He made me scout, give me uniform."[33] This statement is corroborated by an obscure and generally unnoticed letter to the editor of *Desert Magazine* (published in Palm Desert, California, not far from the Salton Sea). The letter tells of a story related by Tom and Tim McCoy, stage coach drivers on the run from Yuma to San Bernardino:

Once in the late '80s Gen. Miles had his military headquarters in Los Angeles. Some of his men, returning from Yuma, lost their way and after much hardship reached Fig Tree's spring near present Fish springs. They were famished for water and might have suffered if the old Indian had not allowed them to drink their fill. He kept them there overnight and sent them on their way. He expressed great admiration for their blue uniforms. Later when new uniforms were issued, the captain of the detail, who had taken a liking to old John, sent his discarded uniform to Fig Tree by messenger. The stovepipe hat was not part of the uniform, but was correct evening dress for that period, and was sent along instead of the regulation cap more or less as a joke.[34]

This story is close enough in the main account of soldiers lost and in need of water to offer support to Juanito Razon's own statement to Brown. I have not been able to trace a military report mentioning this incident or giving the name of the captain — indeed, the incident was probably too minor to have been mentioned in any official reports — but it is true that General Nelson A. Miles was headquartered at Los Angeles in the late 1880s (1887–88 to be exact), and the stage drivers might well have chatted with soldiers going on leave or even with the messenger delivering Juanito Razon's new outfit. It seems safe enough, then, to conclude that Juanito Razon got his first military uniform when he was around 50 years old in return for hospitality and guide services offered to a United States military officer. But that was only the first one.

Actually, Juanito Razon is known to have had several army coats. Photographs show him in at least two quite different ones. People who saw him in his uniform, even in the early days, remember his wearing a very old coat. One Coachella Valley resident in 1974 remembered a trip her husband had made south to the Imperial Valley: "They stopped at Fig Tree John's for water before starting across the dry salt bed. This was before the water came [that is, before 1905]. Fig Tree John made quite an impression on my husband as it was a warm day, but John had on an old army coat. He said it was given to him by an officer of the army who stopped for water. It was worn out, my husband said, a rag, but he always put it on when visitors came."[35]

Another early resident of the area had this to say about the coat: "If I remember right it was in 1906 that some sportsmen stopped at Fig Tree John's place and got a kick out of him. They took him to Los Angeles, dressed him up in a Prince Albert suit, and registered him in a first class hotel. They had a news reporter take his picture and give him a write up in the *Los Angeles Times*."[36] If that story is true, then the Los Angeles coat was probably the second coat, not the first. Still another resident recalled seeing Juanito Razon in the Catholic church on the reservation around 1913: "I can still see that swallow-tailed coat he wore — green with age."[37] Louisa Aguilar recalled the time when Juanito Razon came and asked her father to try to find him a new coat since the old one was worn out. This was no easy task, partly because, even if there were some around, it would have been most difficult to find one small enough to fit Juanito Razon. Her father finally did locate a suitable coat — perhaps a formal evening coat rather than an army coat — and then her mother set about taking it in to fit him and transferring the buttons from an old coat to the new one.

One persistent theory is that Juanito Razon had gotten his original coat from General John Charles Frémont, the famous explorer and army officer, in payment for services as a scout. Though it is remotely possible that this may have been the case, we should remember that no solid evidence for the connection with Frémont has ever been found. Johnny Mack Razon was quite sure that his father had been a scout for Frémont,[38] and Louisa Aguilar also was quite sure. There is reason, however, to be skeptical. No record of a scout named Fig Tree John or Juanito Razon has been found in any documents relating to Frémont. Also, Frémont was not active in the Salton area. The only time he would have come even close to Juanito Razon's area was in 1849, when he was pushing straight west to Los Angeles to meet his wife, who was on her way by ship from Panama. Mary Lee Spence, editor of the Frémont Papers at the University of Illinois, kindly sent me copies of three first-person accounts of this journey: Frémont's own, Thomas E. Breck-

enridge's, and James Stewart McGehee's. None of the three
mentions anything about an Indian who served as guide
across the southern California desert.

I rather suspect that when Juanito Razon first told people about his uniform he had no idea which "general" —
Miles, Frémont, or someone else — was involved, or even
what was the difference between a general and a captain.
Someone may have asked him if it was a gift of the famous
General Frémont, and he may have found that if he said
yes, that impressed them. Frémont was a colorful man who
had become a United States senator from California and
then a candidate for president of the United States. His name
was magic in California, and it was more impressive to claim
to be a Frémont scout than to admit ignorance. One local
resident recalled hearing Juanito Razon "describe the Battle
of San Pasqual, saying that he was there helping the Indians
save the day for Frémont."[39] Since Frémont was not a participant in the Battle of San Pasqual (in 1846), it appears
that Juanito Razon was mistaken, was fibbing, or was misunderstood.

RELATIONSHIP WITH WHITES

Juanito Razon's relationship with whites in the com-
munity is a matter of considerable interest. The record is
ambiguous. On the one hand, he is described as "one of
the best known and beloved of the Indian residents" in the
area,[40] and on the other hand as a suspicious, proud man
who "often resorted to threats of violence to keep unwanted
trespassers off his place."[41] On the one hand he is described
as a harmless old crackpot bluffing his way along with an
empty gun, and on the other he is thought to have murdered
a half-dozen white men.

Juanito Razon's hospitality and generosity to whites
who came to his camp is a matter of record. Frances Anthony
visited him in 1900 and reported that he "assigned us one
of his brush houses, brought us an arm-load of the finest

dry mesquite wood, showed us how to make the fire in the middle of the one room, and pointed out the manner in which the smoke rose to the ridge pole and then went out at the open end. Through it all his manner was as hospitable as any white man's could be."[42] In 1918 Juanito Razon was pleased to see "my good friend, Charley [Brown]," welcomed him to his camp, and gave him a large basket as a present.[43] At about the same time, he shared a watermelon with another white visitor.[44]

Juanito Razon also is known to have saved the lives of more than one lost and thirsty white traveler. Not only do we have the story of General Miles's soldiers referred to previously, but we also have two other specific incidents as well. A young man named "Babe" Smith, undertaking to spend the summer in the desert (apparently prospecting for gold), lost his burros and came crawling into the old man's camp. Juanito Razon nursed the half-dead young man back to health and then took him on horseback to Mecca, ten miles to the north.[45]

On another occasion, in 1913, two great-grandsons of Ulysses S. Grant had automobile trouble in the desert in midsummer. One of the boys, Ulysses S. Grant IV who was then on summer vacation after his sophomore year at Harvard, later published an account of the experience, portions of which are reproduced in the following quotations. On their way south in an Overland automobile along the west shore of the Salton Sea, the two boys stopped for a brief visit at Juanito Razon's spring. They could not find the old man:

This sturdy, primitive orchardist was more commonly known as Figtree John. In a more heroic environment, the unusual appellation "Figtree" attached to his name might have been considered a rude form of heraldry, but in the Salton Basin in 1913, I feel sure it was merely an attempt to distinguish this particular John from all other Johns, of which there were legion. At the time of our visit, Figtree was said to be ninety-one years old, but he was quite spry in spite of the weight of years. His temporary absence permitted us to take an uninvited dip in his quicksand pool.

The boys continued their drive south, but disaster struck when the car broke down. Walking some 20 miles back through the desert heat, drinking only the water drained from the radiator of the disabled car, they finally struggled close to safety before the brother's strength gave out. He waited in the desert while Ulysses went on alone for help and finally arrived at Juanito Razon's spring. This time the old man was in:

Within a few miles, at Agua Dulce, I found Figtree John who, with his squaw and two young boys, was living in a brush and palm leaf ramada. With some difficulty I explained about my brother's predicament and he agreed to go back after him with his team and farm wagon. While the young boys went after the horses, old Figtree carefully greased the much worn axles of his ancient wagon. As the horses walked both ways, it took us over two hours to fetch my brother.

After all these years, I have a clear memory picture of old Figtree John. He was a sturdily built Indian, not tall, but of rugged physique, with very dark skin and a weatherbeaten face, deeply lined by the harsh environment and the scorns of time. His bare feet were like horses' hoofs, and like them, proof against the burns and discomfort of the hot desert sand. His squaw was younger and could have been the mother of the two young boys, who appeared to be around nine years old; but precisely who sired these youngsters, considering John's advance[d] age, may have been a family secret we felt was better left unexplored. After all, we were trespassers on his private domain and he was a dour Indian with a businesslike look around his eyes that discouraged undue inquisitiveness, or indulgence in any form of levity. Tales have been told of his hostility toward travelers but he was friendly to us, though noticeably uncommunicative. It was obvious he had never had any guidance in gracious social living for his table manners were primitive.

According to my diary, Figtree gave us a good supper, consisting of potatoes, noodles, coffee and biscuits. We slept that night on the desert sand beside the shelter. In the morning, our host woke us up at four o'clock, greased the precious wagon axles again, and we started for Mecca. We were so exhausted we both stretched out flat on the floor of the wagon. This trip across the desert to the railroad took three hours, as on sandy desert roads in midsummer horses always walked.

We got to Mecca in time for breakfast at the Hotel Caravansary, a weatherbeaten wooden building with store attached and tents behind for guests. Figtree was our guest for breakfast, disposing of a surprising quantity of food. He was a practical man of small means who grasped any rewards or windfalls that came his way. Later, we saw him at the grocery, investing his pay in copious quantities of starchy foods. Starches are the staff of life of millions of people of slender purse. I fear that the five dollars bonus we gave him for his horses' reward was merely added to his own larder.[46]

DESERT GOLD

This repeated evidence of Juanito Razon's hospitality to white visitors seems to fly in the face of stories that he had murdered a number of white men. To be able to discuss such stories, I must introduce here another whole aspect of his life — his mysterious gold mine.

Recent writers have tended to be skeptical of the stories about Juanito Razon's mysterious gold mine: "There are reliable people who say that he sometimes paid 'Gene' Hill, the pioneer merchant at Mecca, with raw gold. Mr. Hill is dead, and there is no way to prove the report, which has been twisted into all sorts of shapes from the usual lost mine to the myth about a prospector murdered for his gold. If Fig Tree ever had raw gold in his possession, the chances are he received it in payment for a pony or provisions from a prospector or an Indian from the Colorado Indian country where gold was fairly plentiful in early days."[47] A prospector, who once went out on an unsuccessful search for Juanito Razon's supposed mine, concluded that "I rather doubt if the mine exists." He admitted that "some of the aged Cahuillas believe the story of Fig Tree's gold — and that the old Indian killed several trespassers and threw their bodies into the shaft," but he went on to discredit such stories: "Old Fig Tree had a flair for showmanship. He liked to impress the other Indians as much as he did his white neighbors. It is possible the 'mine' was just another story he invented to lend mystery to his strange career."[48] These sound like good common sense responses to still another story of a lost gold mine, but I think we should not be too hasty about dismissing this one.

For one thing, there were those old Cahuillas who believed the story of Juanito Razon's gold. Could he have fooled them? For another thing, those "reliable" people did say he sometimes paid for his supplies with gold. This is corroborated by another statement: "No one seems to question Fig Tree John's easy access to some fountain of great wealth. His existence and his habits were known to at least a few pioneer people. He possessed gold nuggets, and he found them somewhere not too far from where he lived in the 'dry wash' area, now the Salton Sea. When he needed gold he disappeared for three or four days, returned with nuggets in his pockets."[49]

And then there is the tale told about the time that one of the employees of the Southern Pacific Railroad was talking to Juanito Razon in the 1870s about the proposed site for the new railroad. Another white man rode up to the camp and told Juanito Razon and the railroad employee how an Indian squaw from nearby had told him about a certain little black hill to the south of where they were then sitting. This hill was usually covered with sand, but sometimes the wind blew the sand away exposing gold nuggets at the surface. The newcomer had a large nugget which the squaw had given him: "After a long silence, John made a rather cryptic remark. He said, 'Hills don't move, but the place where they are does.' From this it might be interpreted that John knew of the place; that either it was not in the vicinity at all, or else the cagey old Indian was covering up something."[50]

The most interesting account connecting Juanito Razon with gold is the story which an old prospector named H. E. Marshall told to W. A. Linkletter in 1912. Forty years later Linkletter published the account, a few excerpts from which I reproduce below. The story connects Juanito Razon with Pegleg Smith and the famous "lost Pegleg mine."

Thomas L. (Pegleg) Smith was a familiar character around the mining camps of southern California in the Gold Rush days following the discoveries in 1849. He served as guide to several of the early gold-seeking caravans from the East. On one of his trips into the wilderness he discovered

This 1909 picture shows "Gene" Hill's store in Mecca, California. It was said that Juanito Razon paid for supplies here in raw gold which he found or mined in the Santa Rosa Mountains to the west of his home.

his mine. He told several people about it, but never told them where it was. Then, a short time before his death he told his friend, H. E. Marshall — nephew of the Jim Marshall who had first discovered gold in California and started the 1849 gold rush — about the mine. Shortly afterward

Pegleg Smith died. Marshall's efforts to locate the mine
were hampered by his own old age and poor health, by the
terrible desert heat, and by bad luck. Marshall never did
get to the mine, but his account of Juanito Razon's involve-
ment is fascinating:

"Pegleg said he had an Indian by the name of Juanito Razon,
who was afterward Chief of the Agua Dulce Tuba Tribe of
Indians and who was known as "Fig Tree John," guarding the
mine. . . .

"He was getting old and just before he left he gave me a will
to his old Spanish Land Grant on which he said his mine is
located. He gave me a map showing the location of his mine and
also gave to me the half of a talisman which he said fit the other
half that Fig Tree John had. By this talisman and an Indian salu-
tation, which Pegleg told me to greet Fig Tree John with when
I saw him, it was agreed between them that the Indian would
know that I had become the owner of the land grant and the mine.

"Pegleg said the last time he and Fig Tree John were at the
mine, after taking out about two hundred pounds of rich ore, they
had covered up the ledge so no one could find it easily. He was of
the opinion that the desert storms and time had obliterated all
trace of their work and said it would be difficult for me to find
the place where they had taken out the gold without a map and
description so he gave me a map and a complete description of how
to find the mine. . . .

"Fig Tree John was the only living person that has been to
the mine so far as we know. He was sworn by Pegleg never to
reveal the location of the mine and he stolidly refused to tell
anybody where it is. Whenever any one tried to find out from him
where the mine was he came and told me. Before Fig Tree died
a party offered him $500 if he would tell the location of the
Pegleg mine or lead them to it. Several others tried to get some
information from him about the location of the mine but he
refused to give them any.

"Fig Tree John guarded the lost Pegleg mine for years and
it is thought he is responsible for the death and the disappearance
of many prospectors. The skeletons of several prospectors were
found years later and no trace was found of some other prospectors who disappeared while searching for the lost Pegleg mine.
Several years ago a negro prospector was found dead, with a
thirty eight caliber bullet in his body, near Indio. It is said Fig
Tree John was accused of killing the negro and was arrested on

suspicion as he had a thirty eight caliber rifle. I was told a Government attorney was sent out from Washington, D.C., to defend Fig Tree John and he was cleared as the evidence was only circumstantial and nothing was proved against the Indian. . . .

"The negro, who was found dead near his camp at Fish Springs, is said to have taken several thousand dollars worth of 'sunburnt gold' to Los Angeles after his first trip into the desert between Warner's ranch and the Coachella Valley. It was shortly after he had returned to get more of the gold that he was found dead. . . ."

Fig Tree John, with whom the author [Linkletter, not Marshall] is well acquainted, said openly "there is much gold in the mountains near my ranch," but he was never induced to reveal where it could be found.[51]

We must, of course, be highly suspicious of stories about lost gold mines, and of satellite stories about people who were in on the secret but wouldn't tell. Nevertheless, given Juanito Razon's knowledge of the mountains, given the fact that there *was* gold in the Santa Rosas, and given the fact that there is a rather impressive amount of evidence from widely different sources connecting him with gold, it seems quite likely that Juanito Razon knew where to find gold within a couple of days' journey of his home. Convincing corroboration is given in a letter in the Bureau of Indian Affairs files from a woman who tells briefly of the time "old John went with me to show me where there was gold in the hills — but a heavy storm came & he was then over 115 years old & I thought best to turn back. He was never able to take the trip again but told me as near as he could."[52]

As for all those dead prospectors, there is no solid evidence connecting Juanito Razon with any one of them. Surely the desert sun, beating down on men foolish enough to go off alone into uncharted wildernesses, could have accounted for their mysterious disappearance. As for the .38-caliber bullet, other men besides Juanito Razon had weapons which might have fired it, and others besides him might have had a motive for murdering a man who had recently found several thousand dollars worth of gold in the hills. Still, the rumors about the old man's zealous guarding of the gold mine are rather persistent, and they come from a variety of apparently unrelated sources. It is possible that there is some truth to some of them. In one of the stories Juanito Razon is even vaguely rumored to have bragged about doing in prospectors who came too close to his mine:

> The Fig Tree John story intersects the Pegleg Smith saga at one point. After the death of the original Pegleg, a San Jose rancher, said to be a personal friend of the one-legged miner, made camp one day at Seventeen Palms. This is within 15 miles of Fig Tree's spring. The rancher brought with him a 16-year-old boy. On the second morning, he left the camp in charge of the boy, saying he would be back in about four hours. Three days later he had not returned, so the boy reported him missing. San Diego posses searched the area, but no trace of the San Jose rancher was ever found. It was rumored, that Fig Tree John had the job of guarding an Indian mine in the vicinity, and that he had bragged of doing away with prospectors who came near it.[53]

It will probably never be known whether there is any truth to such rumors, and in the absence of proof that Juanito Razon was guilty of murder, it is probably better to assume that he was innocent.

In any event, Juanito Razon's "golden years" appear to have come before he reached retirement age, not after. The stories of his ownership of gold and of his knowledge of the location of specific mines generally refer to his life during the last quarter of the nineteenth century. By the beginning of the twentieth century, when we begin to get firsthand accounts of people who knew him, there are few mentions of gold. Indeed, the most weighty single piece of evidence against the fabulous gold mine theory is that Juanito Razon was apparently not a wealthy man in his last quarter-century. While I think that he must, in his earlier years, have known about the existence of places in the mountains where some of that yellow metal could be found, it appears that those places had probably been pretty well combed of their gold by 1900.

EARNING A LIVING

The records of the last quarter-century of Juanito Razon's life tell the story of a man grubbing for a living, not the story of a man with a rich gold mine in the hills. Perhaps it tells us as much about the interests of white men as it does about the activities of this Indian, but the record of Juanito Razon's economic life is amazingly complete. White observers may not have known what Juanito Razon's feelings were, but they seem, collectively, to have made it their business to know how he made his living. Perhaps this is just an extension of the attitude that makes the second question we almost always ask a new acquaintance — after "How do you do?" — "What do you do?"

Juanito Razon's economic profile was a highly diversified one. He was engaged in the following economic activities between 1905 and 1927:

Agriculture. In 1905, just before the flood, Juanito Razon had a fine orchard of fig trees, "the finest and earliest bearing of the country. The figs are about the size and shape of a turkey egg, and delicious in flavor, being very sweet. They ripen the first of May, and his son ships them to the Los Angeles market at twenty-five cents a pound."[54] He also is known to have raised watermelons, alfalfa, grapes, corn, chickens, horses, and cows.

Manufacturing. Around 1917 Juanito Razon sold to J. Smeaton Chase a horsehair rope he had made himself. The rope was especially valuable, Juanito Razon said, because when it was placed on the ground, a rattlesnake would not cross it. Chase got it at a special price of two dollars because he was a friend. For anyone else it would have cost four dollars.[55] Juanito Razon also sold baskets made by members of his family. He took them to the store to trade for food, or sold them to visitors who came to his camp. A well-made Cahuilla basket could be sold, even in 1905, for ten dollars.[56]

Modeling. There are frequent reports that Juanito Razon charged for letting white men take his picture. Not all reporters tell how much they had to pay, although the usual fee seems to have been a dollar. This was probably a fairly constant source of income, for it has been estimated that during the later years of his life, Juanito Razon was "the most photographed Indian in southern California."[57]

Lecturing. Louisa Aguilar recalls that Juanito Razon would sometimes appear in town for certain occasions and charge tourists for talking about himself, his people, and local history.

Tourism. Cornelia B. White once hired Juanito Razon to accompany her on a long desert trip. She found him to be "a most trustworthy individual, as well as an excellent guide."[58]

Salvage operations. When the Colorado River came rushing down the white man's canal and filled up the Salton Sink, it displaced not only Juanito Razon but also the Southern Pacific Railroad, which had laid its track too low. As the water rose, the tracks had to be moved to the east. In their haste the railroad builders left pieces of track here and there. Juanito Razon salvaged what railroad ties he could. Those he didn't use to build a cabin for himself, he sold to the white ranchers for fence posts.

Equestrian dealings. "In early days he always managed to keep a herd of lean ponies on his rancheria. And he made a good thing out of swapping them. He liked to spend two or three days dickering, getting all the fun and profit that could be squeezed out of a deal."[59]

Grazing leases. In 1917 Juanito Razon arranged with a local rancher, W. F. Beal, to let Beal graze cattle on his lands. Beal was to pay him ten cents per head per month.[60]

Rescue operations. U. S. Grant IV gave Juanito Razon an unspecified amount of money for taking him and his brother to Mecca after their nearly disastrous automobile trip in the desert. Juanito Razon even got a five-dollar bonus to buy a little something for the horses.[61] We may assume that he also got a bit of cash for his rescue of "Babe" Smith.

Geological reclamation. When Charley Brown was wondering where he could get some good gravel to make concrete, Juanito Razon offered to guide him to a place he knew about. They went and found "a bank of gravel so clean and uniform in texture that it could be mixed with his cement just as it was scooped from the ground."[62]

Courtesy Harry C. James

In 1959 Harry C. James took this close-up of what remained of Juanito Razon's cabin in Section 19. The old man had built the cabin after 1906 from railroad ties salvaged from portions of the Southern Pacific Railroad, which was abandoned when the rising Salton Sea forced a relocation of the tracks. At the time the photograph was taken the cabin was used as a storage shed for farming tools, supplies, and equipment.

Welfare. Juanito Razon received for a time a monthly credit allowance from the government at a store near where he lived. This he used for such commodities as "flour, beans, rice, dry salt pork, bacon" and the like.[63]

Water selling. Juanito Razon let motorists fill up their radiators from his spring for a dollar.[64]

Extortion. One local resident told this story about the old man's business habits: "Fig Tree John had his own style of salesmanship. When people came to his place in need of water John would say, 'You buy figs, plenty water. No buy figs, no water.' "[65]

Begging. Sometimes Juanito Razon would call on various white housewives in the area bringing in, say, a watermelon to trade for, say, sugar and coffee. "When he had nothing to exchange, he tried just asking for what he wanted. It often worked. He made a habit of calling about once a week on various housewives and frankly stating what food he craved. Usually he got it."[66] An Indian Bureau official once said that Juanito Razon lived "largely by begging from Desert travelers and workmen or from the local towns people."[67]

Stealing. "Occasionally a white man missed a tool, a bucket or a piece of harness. It was easy to blame Fig Tree John. Sometimes the missing article was seen in Fig Tree's possession."[68]

What may have looked to whites like extortion, begging, and stealing, of course, was probably considered by Juanito Razon to be merely taking his rightful due, a kind of tax or rent to be collected for the use of land which his people had owned for years and of which Chief Cabazon had given him officially documented control. In 1878 Chief Cabazon had said to the Indian agent: "When white brother come, we make glad, tell him to hunt and ride. He say, 'Give me a little for my own,' so we move little way, not hunt there. Then more come. They say move more, and we move again. So many times. Now we are small people, we have little place, but they say move to new place, away from white friends, go out from valley."[69] Juanito Razon was one Cahuilla who, as we shall see, decided he would not move any more. He also decided that he would earn, or demand, or perhaps even steal, what he thought he had a right to from these white men who had taken away so much from his people — and from him.

REAL ESTATE DIFFICULTIES

The white men had, indeed, taken much from Juanito Razon, and this brings us to the old man's extended difficulties in maintaining ownership of his land. To understand why the old man was hostile to some visitors to his camp, and why some of his neighbors complained of his aggressive behavior, we must understand that the lands he claimed as his own, the lands he and his family had lived on for years, suddenly turned out to belong to the Southern Pacific Railroad Company. Previous writers appear not to have known about any of this, probably because most of the documents I shall present in the coming pages, I uncovered only recently in the files of the Bureau of Indian Affairs in Riverside, California, and in the National Archives in Washington, D.C. It is essential to an understanding of Juanito Razon's real estate situation and his resulting behavior that I make clear the rather complicated legal dealings between him, the Bureau of Indian Affairs, and the Southern Pacific Railroad.

As an inducement to the Southern Pacific Railroad Company to lay tracks across the mountains and deserts east of Los Angeles, the United States Government granted to the Railroad Company the ownership of alternate "sections" along a certain width of land on either side of the tracks. A section is one square mile, or 640 acres. In order to prevent the Southern Pacific from amassing huge chunks of land, the United States Government decided to limit the company's potentially monopolistic capacity by granting it only every other section. The rest of the land remained public land to be disposed of by the government through the Homestead Act or by assigning it to Indian reservations, or whatever. The division was made on a quite arbitrary basis, with all the odd-numbered sections along the railroad route going to the Southern Pacific, and all the even-numbered sections remaining in the government's control.

At about the same time that the railroad was receiving its official right to all of the odd-numbered sections along the new train route, President Grant issued an executive order setting aside reservation lands for the Cahuilla Indians in southern California. This all took place in the second half of the 1870s. Since the Southern Pacific Railroad was to go through traditional Cahuilla grounds, what this meant in effect was that the Indians found themselves entitled to live on only half of the lands they had formerly ranged over. That was bad enough in itself; what made it even worse was that the lands were checkerboarded. Each square mile of reservation land was bordered on all four sides by non-reservation land owned by the railroad and was contiguous with other reservation land only at the four corners. The even-numbered sections belonged to the Indians, while the odd-numbered sections belonged to the railroad, which had the right to sell, lease, or otherwise dispose of them. This system may have been an effective check to the power of the railroad, but it did not do the Cahuilla Indians much good, for the assignation of sections was entirely arbitrary, with no care taken that the traditional homes, or even villages, of the Indians be preserved and maintained for their own use. In his annual report of 1881 to the Commissioner of Indian Affairs, S. S. Lawson, agent in charge of the southern California Mission reservations, mentioned several sources of difficulty for the Indians under his control. One of them relates to the checkerboard division of land:

A further source of trouble in this connection is that growing out of the fact that even-numbered sections have been reserved for Indians within the limits of "railroad land grants." In some instances their villages are found to be on railroad sections; or, if they happen to be on reserved land, their little fields, cultivated all these years, are claimed as within the limits of the railroad grant. . . . The lands are entered in the office of the railroad company, taken and occupied, and the Indians turned out. Now if the same rights which attach in common to the *bona fide* white settler occupying land prior to such grant to railroads were accorded to Indian occupants, it would be different; but, unfortunately for the Indian, he has not yet in *fact* come to be considered by the government as a *man,* although bearing the impress of a common Maker in all respects except as to the color of his skin.[70]

It was Juanito Razon's misfortune that he lived in a desert where water was an absolute necessity to survival, and that the two springs he lived at happened to be on odd-numbered sections. His original spring, marked on old maps as "Fig Tree John Spring," was in Section 33. When that was inundated in 1906, he moved north to another good spring he knew about, but that one happened to be in Section 19, another odd-numbered section. Even though both of these sections were a good ten miles away from the railroad tracks, and across the Salton Sea from them, the old man discovered after a time that he was officially just a squatter on private property owned by the Southern Pacific Railroad Company.

After the Southern Pacific Railroad Company received final title to the odd-numbered one-mile-square sections in 1905, its officials decided that to secure effective control over the lands and to make them attractive to buyers or potential lessees, they would have to clear the lands of all Indians living on them. When they came to understand that an old man named Juanito Razon claimed substantial parts of their Sections 19 and 33, and that he refused their requests to leave, they decided that they should try to lease the land to the United States Government for him. They were less interested at that point in the rent money for the lease than in asserting their clear ownership of all of Sections 19 and 33. Accordingly, on October 13, 1913, B. A. McAllaster, Land Commissioner for the railroad, wrote from the main office in San Francisco to C. E. Kelsey, Special Agent for the Indians of California, stationed at San Jose. In the letter McAllaster initiated procedures for leasing the lands in question to the government. Kelsey looked into the matter, and then made his recommendations in a letter to the Commissioner of Indian Affairs in Washington, D.C.: *

---

*For most of the rest of this section, I shall let selected letters speak largely for themselves. The letters are taken from the files of the Bureau of Indian Affairs Agency at Riverside, California, and from the National Archives (Bureau of Indian Affairs file no. 131113–13, California Special 320) in Washington, D.C. Unless otherwise indicated by brackets or by ellipses, all letters are reproduced exactly as written, except that I eliminate headings, file codings, and closings. I reproduce exactly the various small errors of spelling and grammar, but silently correct certain obviously typographical errors (when, for example, a space is omitted between words).

Special Agent Kelsey to Commissioner of Indian Affairs, November 3, 1913

Sir:

For many years an Indian known to most Americans as Fig Tree John, but who claims the name Juanito Razon, has lived in the desert near the northwestern corner of the Salton Sea. Prior to the formation of this lake in 1906 Razon had a field of alfalfa and some very large fig and palm trees. Some of them were killed by the water, which has now subsided below the 200 foot contour below sea level.

Since the passage of the Act of March 4, 1913 Public No. 438, I do not know its position in the Statutes at Large, I have been trying to get a proper description of the lands occupied by Juanito Razon, with the expectation of asking that he receive the benefit of the said Act.

I enclose you herewith a letter received from the Land Commissioner of the Southern Pacific Railroad Co., asking that we remove Razon from the land and offering to execute a lease for the remainder of the year for the sum of $10. I think this had better be done. It will give time to make the request in due form for the exchange and the sum named, $10, is merely a nominal price.

The main spring and three cabins of Juanito Razon are on the NW¼ of Sec. 33, T. 8 S. R. 9 E., S.B.M. A cabin and spring are over the line on the NE¼ of said section. This is according to the statement of certain subordinates of the railroad company, and is probably correct.

According to the railroad people Razon also claims a couple of cabins and springs in the NW¼ of Sec. 19, T. 8 S. R. 9 E., S.B.M. My understanding is that this place belongs to another Indian, who is a son-in-law or some other relative of Razon. This land in Section 19 is valuable. Immediately over the line is the Oasis orange grove of forty acres of naval oranges, now just in bearing. The orange grove is worth probably $50,000. The land occupied by the Indians could be sold by the railroad for probably $100 per acre, as it is artesian land with little frost. The land in Section 33 is less valuable, but worth probably $50 per acre. No artesian wells have been developed, but the springs show an abundant water supply. This is the last water toward Imperial for forty miles. According to the railroad people Razon now lives on Section 19 and has done so since he was driven out by the water. But he goes to sec. 33 about every day and I think he considers it his home. I also enclose a clipping showing how Razon assisted the Grant boys.

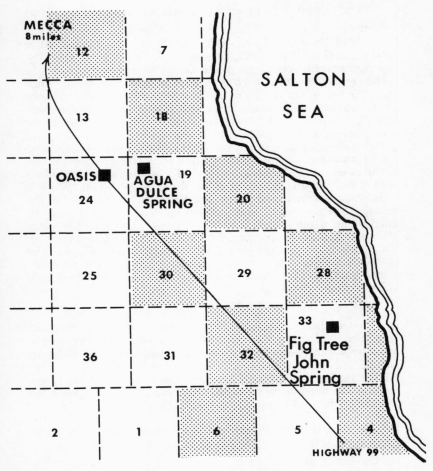

This map shows the "permanent" shore line of the Salton Sea at about
230 feet below sea level. The even-numbered, one-mile-square sections are
shaded to indicate that they were part of the Torres Martinez Indian Reservation. The odd-numbered sections were owned mostly by the Southern
Pacific Railroad Company. The railroad itself is ten miles to the northeast
on the other side of the Salton Sea. When the Salton Sea rose in 1905–07,
Juanito Razon moved from "Fig Tree John Spring" in Section 33 to Agua
Dulce Spring in Section 19. He lived there until his death in 1927.

[The clipping, from an unidentified newspaper, reads as follows:

SAN DIEGO, July 12.—It has just been learned that Chaffee and U. S. Grant the fourth, sons of U. S. Grant Jr. of this city, barely escaped perishing on the desert several days ago. The brothers were on their way in an auto to Imperial valley. When near the Salton sea and 37 miles from Mecca their machine broke down and they were unable to repair it. Their supply of water was soon exhausted and for two days and a night they had none, except some that they drank from the automobile radiator, and which caused Chaffee Grant to become deathly sick. At that time the brothers had tramped over 20 miles across the scorching sands. Chaffee Grant could go no farther. His brother then pressed on alone, making for an Indian cabin three miles distant. When it was reached it required some time to make Fig Tree John, the occupant of the place, understand what was wanted. Finally he hitched up a mule team and accompanied Grant to the place where he had left his brother. They found Chaffee Grant lying on the sands and apparently in a state of complete collapse. The Indian conveyed the Grants to Mecca, where they procured transportation to Los Angeles. They are now fully recovered from their terrible experience.]

I would therefore respectfully recommend that steps be taken to secure for Juanito Razon an exchange with the railroad company by which Razon will secure title to his home and improvements. This land is in the territory of Supt C. T. Coggeshall, of Malki. He will probably be able to inform you the name of the Indians on Section 19. I think they also should be given the benefit of the exchange Act, if possible.

Kelsey's recommendation that the Government exchange other lands with the railroad so that Juanito Razon could stay on the lands he claimed in Sections 19 and 33 was, unfortunately, never carried out. The Commissioner of Indian Affairs wrote to Charles T. Coggeshall, Superintendent of the Malki Indian Agency, giving him instructions to look into the matter. Coggeshall was told to visit Juanito Razon personally and determine whether he had lived on the land in question for at least five years. If he had, then Coggeshall was to make arrangements for a lease with the Southern Pacific Railroad Company for Juanito Razon's use of the land. Superintendent Coggeshall did visit the sections involved, but was unable to find Juanito Razon on the premises. Clearly not at all sympathetic to Juanito Razon's claim to ownership of the land, he sent in the following report:

Superintendent Coggeshall to Commissioner of Indian Affairs, January 13, 1914

Sir:

Referring to Office letter of November 22, 1913, submitting papers rel. to occupation and lease of railroad land in Section 19 and 33 Twp. 8 S. R. 9 E., for an old Indian called "Figtree John" otherwise named Juanito Razon, the Office is informed that I have covered this detail going over the lands in question via automobile, inspecting the buildings, improvements (so called) and taking photographs of same which I herewith submit for the information of the Office. I ascertained that the Indian does not and has not resided on Section 33 for a number of years and there is no improvements on this Section aside from 3 old tumbled down mesquite shacks and 13 fig trees which are all but dead for want of water and have absolutely no cash or other value. The information I have is that Juanito Razon has resided on the NW¼ of Section 19 for a number of years past and his improvements on that quarter Section consists of a few straggly fruit trees that do not bear, a house made of dobe and railroad ties, a brush shelter shack (so called barn and a building that would be termed a chicken house). Former Spl. Agt. Kelsey, is correct in stating that this land is valuable as is shown by the 80 acre orange grove immediately over the line from the buildings shown in the photo marked #1 and just back of same, this grove is easily worth $2,000 per acre as its fruit is fully a month earlier than any of the Riverside County fruit and consequently this grove called the Oasis Ranch brings an average $4.00 per box net.

In as much as it does not appear that this Indian has made his residence on Section 33 for the last few years but to the contrary it does appear that he has taken up residence on the NW¼ of NW¼ of Section 19 Twp. 8 S., R. 9 E., and has expressed his desire to have this land in allotment and for his permanent home, I can see no reason why the Government should lease any part of Section 33 but if it is desired to permit this Indian to hold his present residence a lease should be prepared covering the last and present fiscal year for the NW¼ of the NW¼ of said Sec. 19 Twp. 8 S., R. 9 E., and then later, if the Office desires, steps can be taken with the end in view of obtaining a reconveyance of the said land. Mr. Kelsey is evidently mistaken in his statement that the land on Sec. 19 was occupied by some other Indian as old "Fig Tree John" lives there and owns the buildings occasionally his son stays there with him but claims no part of the so called improvements.

Old Fig Tree is a well-known character in the Desert Country and is mostly famous for refusal to live anywhere near civilization or in anything that approaches a civilized manner, in his younger days he was one of the hardest propositions among the Desert Bands and even now in his old age is not amenable to suggestion or moral suasion and lives largely by begging from Desert travelers and workmen or from the local towns people.

I have several times taken up with Old John his situation and attempted to get him to come onto the Reservation and take up a tentative allotment where he would be near water etc., but he has steadily refused to consider my offers. As a matter of fact there is no reason that I can see as to why the Government should either lease or exchange lands with the Railroad to secure an allotment for this Indian as his improvements do not amount to sufficient cash consideration to pay for a years lease and his agricultural improvements are practically worthless. There is plenty of land that can be tentatively allotted to him on the Torres or Cabazon Reservations where he would be much better off than on either Sec. 19 or 33 as he has nothing on either of these places except over-flow from ranches that lie above Sec. 19 and the reservoir located on this land which is supplied by seepage from small springs and is only sufficient in its present condition for watering stock and domestic purposes.

The Newspaper clipping showing how Old "Fig Tree" assisted the Grant boys may be true but I believe the boys would have been saved had Old John not been on the job, however, to my knowledge I have known of his "standing off" White men on the Desert who wanted water and threatening to shoot if they watered their stock in what he called his reservoir. I herewith submit an affidavit made by two citizens of the Town of Thermal who have known "Fig Tree John" for a number of years and of their own knowledge that he has resided on Section 19 for more than 5 years prior to March 5, 1913. In view of my findings in this matter it appearing that Section 33 has not been occupied by Juanito Razon for years as a residence or anything like a permanent abode, the instructions of the Office are a little to indefinate for me to determine just what sort of lease it is desired be drawn up between the S.P. R.R., and the Government, that is whether it is desired to lease the land on Section 33 or 19 or both for the past year and further I desire the Office to have the facts I have submitted before I take any action in this matter.

If the Railroad Company considered Old John an intruder or desired to use this land why was the matter not brought to my attention by the Officers of the Company. I knew the Indian was on this land and had told him that he had no rights and that none would accrue to him by reason of his residence or otherwise but that he would have to get off whenever ordered to do so by the Company. This Indian wants no restrictions on his actions, mode of life or habits and it is for this reason that he would not take up land on any of the reservations but preferred to live as a hermit remote from his own people and civilization.

I am herewith returning all the papers sent me by the Office together with the photographs and affidavit and would request that I be further instructed as to just what the Office desires me to do in the premises.

Before long McAllaster received his reply from the Washington office, assuring him that Juanito Razon was being dealt with and would offer no further impediment to the railroad:

Second Assistant Commissioner of Indian Affairs to B. A. McAllaster, February 3, 1914

Sir:

This is with reference to your letter of October 14, 1913, addressed to Mr. C. E. Kelsey, relative to the proposed lease of certain land in California which has been occupied by one Juanito Razon, otherwise known as "Fig Tree John".

As Mr. Kelsey is no longer connected with the Service, this matter was taken up with the Superintendent of the Malki Indian School for report. In the light of this report which has just been received it appears that this Indian is a mere squatter on your company's land, has no rights whatever and has been informed by the Superintendent to that effect. Further it appears that this Indian's improvements on said land are practically worthless, not amounting to sufficient cash consideration to pay for a year's lease.

On the other hand there is plenty of land available for tentative allotment to John Fig Tree on certain Indian Reservations in that vicinity where the Office considers he would be far more advantageously situated than at present.

In view of the foregoing, the Office does not deem it advisable by entering into a lease on his behalf, to encourage this Indian in his persistent refusal to accept the opportunities offered him by the Government for bettering his condition.

The grazing lease forms submitted with your letter of October 14, 1913, are returned herewith.

McAllaster was undoubtedly pleased, but wanted some definite assurance that the old Indian actually had physically left the railroad premises. Ultimately the responsibility fell back on Coggeshall:

Assistant Commissioner of Indian Affairs to Superintendent Coggeshall, March 9, 1914

Sir:

With further reference to your letter of January 13, relative to the occupation by Juanito Razon or Fig Tree John of lands belonging to the Southern Pacific Company, you are advised that the Office is in receipt of a letter from Mr. McAllaster, the land commissioner for this road, wherein he says:

"It is assumed therefore that your Department will take immediate steps to remove this Indian from our land, the continued use of which by him without lease is prejudicial to the interest of Southern Pacific Land Company. When you shall have accomplished his removal, will you kindly advise me to that effect?"

Before making reply thereto, the Office wants you to visit this Indian at the earliest practicable date and explain to him the necessity for removing from these lands and locating elsewhere, and that if he fails to take advantage of this opportunity the Southern Pacific Company will no doubt take the necessary legal steps in order to bring about his removal.

When you have carried out this suggestion submit a report showing what action he will take.

Juanito Razon decided that he had better get some professional help if he expected to defend himself against the combined forces of the Southern Pacific Railroad and the United States Government, so he went to see John Brown, a lawyer who lived and practiced in nearby San Bernardino. This was the same John Brown who 20 years earlier had assisted Will Pablo in his campaign to get rid of Agent Horatio N. Rust. Rust had referred to Brown at that time as a "shyster lawyer" who "has been accustomed to advise these Indians for several years (his wife being part Indian), collecting fees and only making the Indian and the agent trouble."[71] Brown helped his new client by writing a letter to Coggeshall on Razon's behalf (letter not in file). Apparently sharing his predecessor Rust's opinion of lawyers who helped Indians, Coggeshall wrote back politely suggesting that Brown should mind his own business:

Superintendent Coggeshall to John Brown, April 11, 1914

Dear Sir:

I am in receipt of a communication from you dated the 10th instant in which you say Juanito Razon, otherwise and better known as "Fig Tree John" has called on you for advice etc., and that you would like to present his case to me etc.

Replying I have to say that I tried to see Juanito Razon when at Martinez on the 6th instant but . . . was unable to . . . , hence, my business with him will have to await my next visit to that place.

Acting under Administrative Office instructions I have a matter to take up with him that needs no outside representative nor does he need any introduction or is there any need of his seeking legal council or other advice than what I, as the Government Agent, have to give him which will be to his best interests. Your advice to Juanito was most excellent and he will do well to follow it, however, the matter I have to take up with him is one wherein he can follow the dictates of his own judgement and if he will accept same my best advice without let or hindrance by me or any of the employees under my jurisdiction.

As Agent I am usually guided by the Administrative head of Indian Affairs and believe in being sure of my position and premises before taking action and should Juanito later seek your advice which I have no doubt he will in his best interests you will advise him to proceed along the lines I have advised him to follow which will be strictly in accordance with my instructions and Governmental directions. I am sure your good judgement and knowledge of the law will carry your actions and intercourse with an Indian people, Wards of the Federal Government and under my jurisdiction, along safe and sane channels and thus we may avoid friction or trouble for I assure you, my dear Sir, as I think I advised another of your name, as the authorized Government Agent of this jurisdiction any attempt misrepresent, collect fees, or disturb the peace and tranquility of the United States in this Indian Country will be severely dealt with under the United States laws.

The "matter" to which Coggeshall alluded in the last letter was a proposal designed to make it attractive for the recalcitrant old Juanito Razon to move from railroad land onto the reservation proper by providing a new well on the reservation section. Acting on the advice of his agent, his lawyer, and his son, the old man agreed:

Superintendent Coggeshall to Commissioner of Indian Affairs, May 20, 1914

Sir:

Referring to Office letter of March 9, 1914, in the above given case of old "Fig Tree John" or Juanito Razon one of the Martinez Indians living on Railroad land, I have to report that I have made several efforts to see this Indian dating back to my receipt of Office letter of instructions but that until the 19th inst., was unsuccessful in locating him. Tuesday the 19th I had an interview with his son known as "Johnnie Mack" also a nephew of Juanito and I took up this matter with them explaining to them the situation that they were living on Railroad lands and had no right thereto or to residence thereon and that unless they peacefully gave up the land and removed therefrom, the Railroad would forceably remove them if necessary after taking such legal action as lay with them under the circumstances.

Johnnie Mack is the mouth-piece of his Old Father Juanito Razon who is one of the old time Indians and whose ideas are rather confused and jumbled and who usually appeals to some legal Shark whenever anything comes up that he is unable to grasp mentally and he is consequently rather a hard proposition to deal with unless it be through one of his sons who have some little education and knowledge of business matters etc.

It appears that Johnnie Mack was authorized by his father to take up this matter with me and ascertain the status of the situation and pass judgement, therefore, after explanation to Johnnie and telling him, as I had told both he and his father 2 years ago, that they could take up land on the Reservation etc., he said they would take up land on Section 2 south of Alimo Indian Village and would clear up a piece of same if I could get them water. I advised Johnnie that I understood the Irrigation Indian Service contemplated extensive development of the Desert Reservations this next fiscal year and that I would write the Commissioner about this matter and I was most confident that when this development was made that a well would be put down for him and his father, Juanito Razon, and I would invite attention to it later and personally recommend it etc.

As I expected Juanito Razon made a trip to San Bernardino to see a Lawyer by the name of John Brown, Jr., and put this case before him. Brown is known as the "Indian Lawyer" and to my knowledge is an excellent friend of the Indians if there is anything to be made out of them in the way of fees etc. I received a letter from this man saying he would like to present the case of "Juanito Razon" to me etc., to which I replied that I was here to look after the interests of these Indians and that those of Juanito needed none of his attention; that I would take up whatever business I had with Juanito direct and that I would advise him, Mr. Brown, to attend strictly to his own particular business and not attempt to extort fees through any misrepresentations or otherwise from an Indian, Ward of the Federal Govt., under my care and jurisdiction, to this letter I have not received any reply and as I further advised Mr. Brown that the best advice he could give Juanito would be to tell him to be guided by my advice which would be altogether in his interests as his friend and welwisher, I guess from what I gathered at the recent conference Mr. Brown must have conveyed this advice.

The Office may safely advise the Railroad Company that Juanito will vacate their lands and move onto the Reservation in the near future or whenever they send him word in case they desire them vacated at once. I believe that if they desire an immediate removal word through some representative of the Railroad would be more effective than any other method of urging the matter as I have Johnnie Macks' word that they will remove peacefully and on receipt of notice from the Railroad believe they would move at once. However, if the Office desires that I move them or cause their removal, I will on receipt of such instructions see that they vacate within a reasonably limited time allowing them time in which to gather their possessions and make proper removal.

This last letter shows that Juanito Razon was, after all, willing to listen to a reasonable offer. If he could be assured of an adequate water supply, he would move to land on a reservation section and relinquish his claim to the lands in Sections 19 and 33. Three months later, however, after an exchange of letters about how Juanito Razon was to be removed from the land, the old man was still there:

Superintendent Coggeshall to B. A. McAllaster, August 21, 1914

Dear Sir:

Regarding your letter of the 13th instant in re. the removal from the Southern Pacific Companies lands of an Indian named Juanito Razon, otherwise known as "Fig Tree John" you are advised that I have notified this Indian that he was tresspassing on lands not the Governments' and that he should remove his belongings, buildings and himself and family and move onto the Govt. reservation under the Martinez Subagency or he would lay himself liable to prosecution and possible trouble etc.

A son of old John's advised me that "Fig Tree" would do this and to the best of my knowledge and belief he fully intended that his father would take this action, however, Old Fig Tree is as amenable to suggestion as the proverbial Government mule and has a reputation of being a bad actor in former years and I am informed that he still occupies your lands.

I was directed to take the matter up with John and tell him to move etc., however, my instructions did not direct me to use force in this matter and I am of the opinion that there is no law under which I could forcably remove this man from lands not the Governments' and force him to take up residence on the Reservation against his free will. I understand that Juanito has placed this matter in the hands of an Attorney by the name of John Brown, Jr., of San Bernardino, Calif., and that he has stated that he will not move etc. Therefore, it appears to me that the proper course for you you to pursue is to take action legally to secure an order for his removal in the proper State Court and have same served by a duly authorized State officer.

I am further taking the matter up with the Indian Bureau in Washington and without the Bureau through its Administrative head directs me to forcibly remove this Indian from your lands in the absence of any law under which I would be justified in taking such action, I must refuse to take other than such acts of moral suasion as I have already employed to accomplish the results desired.

Coggeshall did not mention the reason for Juanito Razon's refusal to move. Three months later McAllaster, of the railroad company, found out the reason: the well was never drilled, so Juanito Razon would have had no water on the lands he and his sons had already begun to clear. McAllaster suggested that the lease question be explored again:

B. A. McAllaster to Assistant Commissioner of Indian Affairs, December 2, 1914

Dear Sir:

Referring to yours of October 7, 1914, concerning the occupancy of certain Southern Pacific Land Company Land in the vicinity of Mecca, California, by Juanito Razon or Fig Tree John, beg to advise that we have lately been negotiating with this Indian in the effort to obtain his peaceable removal from the land.

He has been making preparations to move onto the Indian Reservation, but just as his arrangements were complete the Indian Agent informed him that there were no funds available to drill a well for him on the site on the reservation selected by him. Mr. Nichols, who I understand is connected in some manner with the Indian Bureau, has corroborated his statement and says further that he has no idea when the necessary money will be available.

In the light of the fact that the Indian Bureau cannot properly take care of this Indian and his family on a Reservation at the present time, it would seem to me that you should arrange to take a lease on our land covering such period as will presumably elapse until proper provision can be made for accommodating him on the Indian Reservation.

Will you kindly look into the matter further and either arrange for his immediate accommodation on the reservation or advise me that a lease will be taken by the Indian Bureau for his benefit and the term which you desire such lease to cover, whereupon I will draft a proper lease, following the form heretofore used in making leases of lands to the United States for like purposes, and submit the same to you for approval.

Coggeshall was asked to look into the matter once again. Convinced that the Indians were acting in good faith, he recommended that arrangements be made for a lease:

Superintendent Coggeshall to Commissioner of Indian Affairs, January 29, 1915

Sir:

Referring to Office letter of December 14, 1914, in re. a letter which was enclosed by the Office received from Mr. B. A. McAllaster of the Southern Pacific Land Company, Dec. 3, 1914, I have to say that I have deferred making a reply to this letter until I could locate the Indians effected and interview them in regard to this land etc., and that having visited the son of old "Fig Tree" today I can now report intelligently on this matter.

To begin with the Irrigation Service of Los Angeles under whose supervision the irrigation work in this district comes advise me that nothing can be done toward putting down a well and furnishing water to old "Fig Tree" until sometime after the passage of an appropriation bill making specific appropriation for work under the Martinez district. This being the case, I believe it might be proper and but right in the interests of these Indians that old "Fig Tree" be permitted to remain on the lands of the S.P. Land Company until such time as he can be furnished a well on the land he has selected on the Torres Reservation. His son, called "Johnnie Mack" otherwise known as John Razon, has cleared up something over 5 acres in the extreme southern end of this reservation, he desires to go into fruit raising oranges etc., and the land selected is admirably suited for this industry, however, he and his father "Fig Tree" can do nothing with the land until water is furnished them which calls for the boring of a well on the land they have cleared.

They are both agreeable to move onto the reservation and relinquish the lands of the Railroad Company whenever they are furnished water on the reservation lands they have cleared and they will then do more development work and clear a much larger area etc.

In view of these facts and the fact that they both express a wish to retain use of the S.P. Land Company's land until such time as water can be supplied them, I would recommend the drawing of a lease covering the land of the Land Company on which they are located said lease to run for a term expiring with the calander year 1915 by which time it would appear that money would have been available for development work at Martinez and that the need of these Indians could be attended too. I would suggest that a note be made of the need of this particular well and the Irrigation Service through Supt. C. R. Olberg be requested to give this particular Indian attention among the first work to be done here, this action will obviate the necessity of drawing out the leasing period and will also do justice to the Indians concerned and place them in a position to become self supporting and develop the land selected in the manner they desire which appears to me to be most commendable and is to my personal knowledge of this particular parcel of land an industry in which they should be encouraged.

There followed a series of letters concerning the details of the lease, but it was finally approved by the Bureau of Indian Affairs on October 18, 1915. And so, a full two years after it initiated the request, the Southern Pacific Railroad Company secured its lease for lands to be used by Juanito Razon in Sections 19 and 33. The rent agreed upon by the United States Government was ten dollars a year for the 422 acres involved. This rent was scarcely worthwhile from a financial standpoint for the railroad, but the lease did establish the railroad's ownership of the land, and that was all it desired. Juanito Razon became a renter, which was better than being a squatter, but not as good as being an owner.

After more than a year of living on the land leased for him, Juanito Razon was paid a visit by John J. Terrell, Special Commissioner to the Indians of California. Terrell was apparently trying to determine whether the lease should be renewed. His letter reporting to the Commissioner of Indian Affairs in Washington provides a number of valuable details about Juanito Razon's life. I have deleted sections of the letter which result from Terrell's misunderstanding of the location of some of the leased lands. It seems that he had been told that the government was leasing lands in Sections 19 and *23*, not 19 and *33*. This puzzled Terrell because Section 23 was entirely submerged by the Salton Sea and so was utterly useless to Juanito Razon. He recommended that the government seek a rebate for rent paid in the past for this useless land. Because of this unfortunate error, Juanito Razon lost his claim to ownership of his original home on Section 33. Terrell was, however, very sympathetic to the old man's rights to lands in Section 19. Probably because Juanito Razon saw the necessity to establish residence on one piece of the land, he told Terrell that he was born on Section 19, although in truth he had moved there, already an old man, only ten years earlier:

Special Commissioner Terrell to Commissioner of Indian Affairs, January 16, 1917

Dear Sir:

   ... I reached the little shack home of old Fig Tree John, which as indicated on the sketch, is situated near the northwest corner of Section 19 said Township and Range, shortly after sunset on the 13th, instant, there being no one at home his thatched squat being securely pad-locked. I pitched camp in his yard, anticipating that he would likely return during the forenoon following day, in that his cats and chickens indicated a temporary absence. He failing to return by about ten o'clock, and learning from a nearby white neighbor that one of his sons lived some four miles to the north, after making a general survey of his place and improvements, noting its proximity to the Salton Sea, proceeded to his son's place finding he and his old full blood wife there.

Old Fig Tree John is a very old typical full blood Indian of the Coahuella Mission Tribe, unable to speak other than his native language, which seemed to be a mixture more or less of the peon Mexican language. He claims to be 97 years of age, and while he bears every mark of age, would judge him between 80 and 90 years old. His old wife, also a full blood, looks equally as old. They have had eight children, five dead and three living, two sons and one daughter, all grown-up and with large families. These two very old people seem remarkably well preserved.

Old John through an interpreter, a young bright educated Indian by name of Ramon, insisted that he and his old wife and all their children, until death or their marriage took them away, continuously lived upon as a home said Section 19, and therefore, same belong to him and his children, after death of himself and wife. I explained to him that under the record and laws of California both sections 19 and 23 said Township and Range belonged to the railway company. This information seemed very displeasing to both he and his old wife.

I find that old John owns only five head of cattle, his only horse having been recently killed, evidently by hunters, since which he has secured and posted the usual printed warning against hunting on "Indian lands."

Evidently this old Indian's parents were attracted in the very early times to the cluster of three springs located . . . near the northwest corner of said Section 19, if in fact old John is correct about being born on this land. The fact of the springs located in a desert country is very suggestive of Indian habitation from the earliest history of these people or even of their earliest existence in that desert land.

This old Indian has erected a one wire fence, comparatively new, possibly of total length about ¾ mile on said section 19 and section 18 adjoining to the north, but not a complete enclosure. . . . His residence or squat home is a very primitive typical Indian affair consisting of posts driven into the soft sandy soil weather-boarded with tula canes, palm leaves, etc, dirt floor and batton door. . . .

There is fairly good grazing on said sections 18 and 19, said 18 being Indian land. The greater necessity for leasing the Northwest Quarter of said Section 19 is to control the three small springs and protect this old Indian's improvements.

These three springs on section 19 appear of near equal volume and value, which if properly cleaned out and their waters conserved, would likely irrigate between one-half and one acre of land each. Old John has some 8 to 10 fairly good size fig trees, 3 or 4 short rows of grapes, small garden patch and also about half acre last season in corn. . . .

After studying the matter, Terrell decided that continuing the lease was contrary to the best interests of Juanito Razon, whose claim to his lands in Section 19, at least, was superior to that of the Southern Pacific Railroad Company. It must have been a very happy day for Juanito Razon and his family when he received the following letter from Terrell telling him that he was the rightful owner of the land:

Special Commissioner Terrell to Fig Tree John, March 28, 1917

Dear Chief, John:

I am much pleased to be able to tell you in this letter that the Indian Office at Washington, D.C., among other things, has to say,

"It is believed that your occupancy long antedates the filing of the railway company's map of definite location, viz; January 31, 1878. This department has held in the case of Ma-gee-see v. Johnson (30 L. D. 125), that where lands are in occupation, possession and use of Indian inhabitants they are not unappropriated public lands. In this connection also see the case of the Northern Pacific Railway Company v. Wismer (230 !ed. Rep. 591). In that case the Circuit Court of Appeals for the 9th circuit held, on February 7, 1916, that A tract of land which on October 4, 1889, when the Northern Pacific Railway Company filed its map of definite location, was within a larger tract than actually occupied by a tribe of Indians (Spokane) under an agreement made with representatives of the Interior and War Departments, subsequently ratified, setting it apart as their reservation, which it continued to be until 1910, was not on such date public land free from pre-emption or other claim within the grant to the railroad company of July 2, 1864 (13 Stat. 365) and did not pass thereunder.

"In consideration of the foregoing, this Office does not deem it advisable to enter into any further lease on behalf of Fig Tree John covering lands in Sections 19 or 23 of said Township 8 South, Range 9 East, SBM., California."

In my report to the Indian Office at Washington on January 16, 1917, the fact that you with your family had lived your entire lives upon this land, and that likely, your parents before you had done likewise, has caused the Office to inform Mr. B. A. McAllaster, Land Commissioner of the Southern Pacific Railway Company at San Francisco, California, as indicated above. This suggests that you should not think of abandoning the land or entering into any kind of an agreement with any one claiming the land and should any steps be undertaken to in any way dispossess you of this land, that is, put you off, that you at once advise the United States Indian Superintendent, at Banning, California.

I would further suggest that you make every possible effort to fence and put more land in cultivation on your home section 19, and if possible make further house improvements, and in this connection request your sons and other relatives to help you.

I am giving your Superintendent at Banning and the Indian Office at Washington advantage of a carbon copy of this letter.

[I hope] that you may spend many happy days, even years, in your home on this section 19, even until you shall be called to the "happy hunting grounds."

What was meant to be a solution to Juanito Razon's troubles, however, turned out to be merely a cause of further difficulties for him. The central problem was that Terrell had not specified, either to Juanito Razon or to the railroad officials, exactly which acres on Section 19 were the rightful property of the old man. When Juanito Razon tried to follow Terrell's enthusiastic but vague advice that he should "fence and put more land in cultivation," he found himself in inevitable conflict with white neighbors who wanted, and who had paid for legal title to, those same lands. McAllaster, the beleaguered Land Commissioner for the railroad, found that Juanito Razon was still giving him headaches, for he received the following letter from Charles S. Sanderson, a white pioneer who was beginning to carve a ranch out of the desert near Juanito Razon's land:

Charles S. Sanderson to B. A. McAllaster,
December 16, 1919

Dear Sir:

I was in to your L.A. Office today to see what steps could be taken in regard to "Old Fig Tree John" — I guess that is the name he goes by — he lives down on your lands near the Oasis Farm by the Salton Sea. You will see by your books that I have paid you some $10,000.00 for land in Sec. 29, Twnp. 8 S. R. 9 E. (240 acres). I am now getting material on ground for a 12 in. well — will spend in the neighborhood of $5000.00 on the well — we have built a small house for the workmen, and have already shipped $2000.00 pipe down and more to follow. My well borer on the ground writes me that the old Indian living near there is making it hot for them — he claims all that country, says it is his old home — the driller wrote to the Indian Agt. who came down and I think must have had some talk with the Indian then came over and told the driller he "must look out for the old Indian." That seems to me rather shifting the burden of police work — I am fearfull if we do not get something better — that I will not be able to go ahead with the improving I have in hand as my men may not care to stay if the Indian is a tough character. We find it very expensive pioneering down there at best — a lot of cash will necessarily have to be expended before results. Some of my friends are contemplating further purchase of your lands in view of my work — this will all stop if we undergo any serious trouble down there. Personally, I think the Government Agt. should have the means at hand to entirely satisfy this old Indian, and at same time make him understand he must keep off our lands where he has started this trouble, I will instruct all the men I have any control of to treat him fair — be *considerate,* and never at any time ridicule or in least way insult him. They naturally will need to be firm and try to make him keep his distance, he seems to think he owns *all* the land that is near him. I realize the difficulty of teaching an old Indian anything — it is no "layman's" job — too much for me. But the Agt. should be equal to it. I am writing this as I feel you will be interested, and from your position you can get in touch with those that *can* handle the situation and to that end I am asking your aid in this matter — it might end more serious than any of us would care to have it. . . .

In this case McAllaster referred the matter to one of the Southern Pacific Railroad Company lawyers, who filed an official complaint at the Indian Bureau in Washington. From

Washington came instructions to Robert E. Burris, the new Superintendent of the Malki Agency, to investigate the validity of Sanderson's complaint. Superintendent Burris's report on the matter showed that he was not inclined to take seriously, much less to interpret generously, Terrell's letter to Juanito Razon, this obdurate "nuisance in the neighborhood." Burris's letter, in effect, reversed Terrell's, for it stated that the land Juanito Razon was living on belonged to others who, if he continued to annoy them, "might eject him at any time":

Superintendent Burris to Commissioner of Indian Affairs, March 23, 1920

My dear Mr. Commissioner:

Relative to communication addressed to your office regarding the conduct of an Indian under this jurisdiction known as "Fig Tree John" I beg to report that previous to the receipt of your letter, I had made three trips on different occasions to see this Indian at his home — which is almost to the Salton Sea — as it had been reported he was a nuisance in the neighborhood. I endeavored to explain to him that he had no right to the land in question and told him repeatedly that he *MUST* cease disturbing the people occupying the land. I told him, as a matter-of-fact the very land on which he has his home is not owned by the Government and that if he continued to annoy the owners they might eject him at any time. I thought I had finally convinced him of the error of his way when a few days later in the "Riverside Enterprise" — the daily newspaper of Riverside — was published a column and a half report of his visit to Jonathan Tibbitts home, where he had gone to consult him about the matter. This clipping I forwarded to the Office with a lengthy report of the activities of Mr. Tibbitts.

Shortly after Fig Tree John's return home he again began to molest the people on the adjoining land and upon it being reported to me I again went down to see him. He then informed me that he "owned all the surrounding country" and his friends in Riverside were to get it back for him. He also produced a letter (citation Land-Allot. 131113–13, 6670–17 PBM, signed by Special Commissioner J. J. Terrell) as his authority from Washington. I carefully and patiently explained the situation, both through an Indian interpreter and talked to him myself in Spanish, which he understands perfectly. After spending the better part of the day at his place I left with his promise to stay away from the adjoining land and that he would "not trouble the people until his friends in Riverside got them moved.". . .

However, until the recent meetings at Mr. Tibbitts place, old Fig Tree John was comparatively quiet but when all the disgruntled trouble-making Indians were sought Fig Tree John was found and taken into the fold. At one time he even threatened to fence and close the public highway which passes in front of where he makes his home — probably would have done so except from the income he derives from motorists who fill their radiators there at $1.00 each.

I am returning herewith all papers sent me and would request that I be further instructed as to just what the Office desires me to do in the premises; that is, just what steps I am to take with Fig Tree John if he continues to be obdurate. It is not likely he will be amenable to suggestion or moral suasion.

After that, perhaps while waiting (in vain) for his friends in Riverside to get the white neighbors moved, Juanito Razon seems to have lived in relative peace and security at his spring on Section 19. Meanwhile, the General Allotment Act of 1887 was being applied on the Torres Martinez Indian Reservation. The Allotment Act provided for Indian reservations, upon the authorization of the president of the United States, to be subdivided and distributed to individual Indians. The idea was that each Indian would more quickly become "civilized" and become worthy of full citizenship in the United States if he could own his own land rather than use land held in common by his tribe. (The idea was also, incidentally, to open up for sale to white settlers all reservation lands not allotted to individual Indians.) The Act provided strict rules for distribution of the land. Each head of a family was to receive a deed to one-quarter of a section (160 acres); each single person over 18 years of age was to receive one-eighth of a section; and so on. Careful provision was made for the Indians to select their own lands from those available on the reservation. Juanito Razon, however, refused to make a selection of on-reservation land. He would stay where there was water, where he had buildings, where he had fruit trees, and where he had lived for the last couple of decades.

Juanito Razon probably did not know that in the General Allotment Act special provision had been made for indi-

viduals like him who would not cooperate by selecting portions of reservation land: "If any one entitled to an allotment shall fail to make a selection within four years after
the President shall direct that allotments may be made on
a particular reservation, the Secretary of the Interior may
direct the agent of such tribe or band . . . to make a selection for such Indian, which selection shall be allotted as in
cases where selections are made by the Indians, and patents
shall issue in like manner."[72] Apparently without his coop-
eration or consent, Juanito Razon was granted an individual
allotment of land on November 16, 1922, amounting to
slightly more than 40 acres. This was less than one-tenth
the amount he had received in the lease from the railroad
company. Worse yet, the land deeded to him was in Section
28, to the south and east of Section 19, and to the north of
Section 33. Juanito Razon never moved onto the land he
was allotted, probably because there were neither houses nor
water on the land. He stayed on at Agua Dulce in Section
19, legally or illegally, until his death from influenza in April
of 1927. By then he was an American citizen; three years
earlier the United States Congress had passed a law making
all American Indians citizens of the United States.

At the time of his death his three children inherited one-
third shares each of the 40-acre allotment in Section 28. They
also attempted to establish their right to inherit the land
occupied by their father in Section 19, and there is considerable correspondence in the Bureau of Indian Affairs files
regarding this matter. Since much of this material relates
only indirectly to Juanito Razon himself, I include here only
two letters regarding the matter. The first is a report made
by the District Superintendent in Charge of the Mission
Indian Agency, Charles L. Ellis, which pretty well sum-
marizes the situation:

District Superintendent Ellis to Commissioner of Indian Affairs, February 14, 1928

Sir:

Reference is made to Office letter of Jan. 3, above reference,
regarding land claimed by Fig Tree John, now deceased, in Secs.
19 and 33 T8S R9E.

The lands in question are claimed by the Southern Pacific Land Company and a part of these sections are now being occupied by white settlers who claim right by reason of contract for deeds from the Southern Pacific Land Company. These settlers are now improving the land by clearing off brush, and plowing and leveling. A well is being drilled in Sec. 19. The present depth is about 300 feet and the white occupant intends to dig deeper.

The farmer at Torres-Martinez, Mr. Humbargar, reports that Fig Tree John lived in Section 19, when he first assumed work at that reservation, Dec. 1, 1922, and that he lived on Sec. 19, until his death which occurred April 11, 1927. Mr. Humbargar made a careful investigation and reports it as his belief that Indian occupancy antedated the grant to the Southern Pacific Company. This is borne out by the testimony of Indians. There are ornamental palm trees now growing around the springs on the land. Only a guess can be made as to the age of the trees but they are evidence of early occupancy by Indians.

Chappo Alimo, an ancient of the Torres-Martinez band, states that he planted the trees on Section 19, 40 or 50 years ago, and contends that the Indians occupied the land years and years ago. Several others claim that the lands were occupied by their parents and grand-parents.

A meeting with the Indians was held Feb. 7, 1928, to learn, if possible, whether Indian occupancy antedated grant to the Southern Pacific Land Company. Chappo Alimo, who claims to be at least 100 years of age, says that Fig Tree John first moved to sections 19 and 33, at the time the water filled the Salton Sea. Alimo states he was a young man, — had a moustache — when the Union Pacific Railroad was built through the Valley, and that Fig Tree John was occupying the land prior to that time. He also stated that other Indians were occupying Sec. 19 and 33, mentioning specifically He-mul-went (Cross Nose) and Pa-le-wet, the grand-father of Basket Chihuahua an Indian who is now living at Torres-Martinez. Alimo says there were a number of other Indians occupying the two sections and adjoining land, but that an epidemic of smallpox caused the death of a number and that some of the survivors left.

Jake Razon and John Mack Razon, sons of Fig Tree John, support this testimony. Jake Razon does not know his age but contends that his father lived on the land prior to the coming of the railroad. John Mack Razon states he is about 55 years of age; that there was a railroad through the Valley ever since he can remember, but that his father was occupying the land. Bernardo Segundo, a Los Coyotes Indian, says he was about 15 years of age when the railroad was built, and that Indians were occupying Sec. 19 and 33 at the time, and had occupied the lands prior.

From what I can learn, it appears the Indian actually occupied and possessed Sec. 19 and 33 prior to the coming of the railroad. Chappo Alimo has the best knowledge, but Bernardo Segundo's statement is considered reliable. The Palm Trees on Sec. 19 were planted in part by Chappo Alimo and look as if they were 40 or 50 years old. Further, the explanation of Alimo as to the reason for the exodus of the Indians — smallpox — is logical and undoubtedly true, Fig Tree John and a few others remaining. Further, the fact that there were springs of living water made this place an oasis which the Indians could not afford to ignore even during an epidemic.

Testimony as to occupancy and use of the land must come from the ancients of the tribe, men of advanced years. They insist the land was occupied by Indians and from what I can learn they are correct in their statements. Any action taken should be commenced in the near future so that the aged Indians, who alone have definite knowledge, can testify.

The Commissioner felt, however, that this report did not demonstrate sufficient grounds for a suit against the Southern Pacific Railroad Company. What was needed was conclusive proof, not just that Indians had lived on the lands in question, but that Juanito Razon himself was occupying one specific home place before 1878 and that he had maintained continuous occupancy on it until his death. The conclusive proof was never found, partly because Juanito Razon had lived on Section 33 only until 1906, and then moved to Section 19, and so had not maintained continuous occupancy on either one; partly because it would have been difficult to establish conclusive proof even if he had not been forced to move by the rising Salton Sea; and partly because his son, Jake Razon, quite understandably, became angry that such legalistic barriers were placed between Juanito Razon's heirs and their rightful due. Having already written letters, answered questions, and signed affidavits, Jake became convinced that further efforts on his part were futile. In the end he had to settle for his third of the forty acres in Section 28. Over a year later Mrs. C. D. Brauckman, a resident of Mecca, wrote to H. E. Wadsworth, Special Allotment Agent, in what was a final — and futile — plea to secure the rights of the heirs to Juanito Razon's homelands:

Mrs. C. D. Brauckman to Special Agent
H. E. Wadsworth, July 8, 1929

Dear Sir:

I suppose you have heard of "Fig Tree John" now deceased. His 2 sons & 1 daughter are very ignorant and have not been cared for as I think they should. They have been trying to get the "Rancho" John left but R. R. claimed & sold it. One of the sons did not take or let his children take their allotment & as I understand the Ranch he has been living on & cultivating is allotted to some one else. This son Jake is considered lazy by the whites but *I know he is not.* He hurt his back in 1908 bailing hay & would not let a *Dr* see him or have any treatment but Indian & never got over it & he can get "boch" to get drunk on when ever he wants to which is not often. Old John was proud of the fact his tribe never fought the whites. If there is any way you can straighten things out for them I know they will appreciate it but *naturally* they do not trust a white man. They will do about what I tell them to & trust me so far that old John went with me to show me where there was gold in the hills — but a heavy storm came & he was then over 115 years old & I thought best to turn back. He was never able to take the trip again but told me as near as he could so you know they have faith in me doing right by them.

I do hope you can help them some way. A Mr Brown — atty of San Bernardino tried but seems failed to get any satisfaction & the Farmer at Martinez Mr Bengratter tried also to do what he could. But some of the Indian agents here have had no use for Indians & Indians have lost what little faith they had. One agent made no secret of saying Indians were no better than dogs & should be treated as such.

Even though some agents and some neighbors treated Juanito Razon as if he were no better than a dog, the old man himself always stood up heroically for his rights as a human being. He had an unusually firm opinion about just what his rights were. We have already seen that he insisted on certain boundary rights, both for his village and for his own homelands around his spring. When he had difficulties, he consulted a lawyer. When he knew he was in the right, he stood firm and refused to move for anyone. One Coachella Valley resident told me about the time road builders were putting in a road on the reservation: "The road was to go through a small grove of fig trees, but Fig Tree John would *not* let them disturb the trees."[73] Finally the workmen diverted the road around the grove.

Louisa Aguilar told me how Juanito Razon would demand "free" rides on the Southern Pacific Railroad. It seems that the railroad officials had promised that in exchange for letting the railroad go through certain Indian lands, the Indians could ride free on the trains whenever they wanted to. As far as she knew, Juanito Razon was the only Indian who ever tried to collect on this promise. It would have taken no small measure of courage for the little man in his top hat and old army coat, speaking imperfect English, to demand, from a ticket agent or a conductor who may never have heard of that promise, the right to a "free" ride to Banning to visit his relatives. He did it though.

Juanito Razon's heroic refusal to be cowed by the officials of the United States Government and of the Southern Pacific Railroad Company is clear evidence that he fought for his rights in the political as well as the personal arena. Lowell Bean wrote of the old man's association with the Mission Indian Federation: "I do not know exactly what his connection with the Mission Indian Federation was except that he was at many meetings. The Mission Indian Federation was a voluntary association, which organized to protest Bureau of Indian Affairs rule over southern California Indians. They attempted to set up an independent political organization — their own police, judges, captains, etc. They published a magazine, were active in lobbying locally and in Washington regarding Indian affairs. They started in 1919, were very strong until World War II."[74] Juanito Razon, then, had a clear idea of his rights as an individual and as an Indian, and he insisted that his neighbors, however powerful they were, respect those rights.

Trying to reconstruct Juanito Razon's life, nearly fifty years after his death, and from whatever documents and recollections are available, is a little like trying to figure out what the dimensions of a sawed plank were by looking at the sawdust, slabs, and ends left at the sawmill after the plank has been shipped. Careful studying and fitting together of such leavings can never be quite like looking at the original, but they can tell us something. In this case, we can say that Juanito Razon was probably in many ways a rather ordinary Cahuilla. He lived his life as best he could and for as long as he could off the land. When he found himself closed in by blue waters and white farmers, he had to build a couple of fences of his own and adjust his way of life somewhat, but he managed.

What set Juanito Razon off from his fellow Cahuillas was that he stood his ground a little more firmly and a little longer than most of them did, that he insisted on his own ways and habits a little more strongly than they did, that he demanded and got a little more from the white man than they did, and that he was a little surer than most of them were that he was just as good as a white man. White men took from Juanito Razon his land, his orchard, his water, his hospitality, his picture. They seem, however, never to have touched his pride.

FIG TREE JOHN

IN FICTION

A PROUD APACHE

There have been four paperback editions of Corle's Fig Tree John. *The first (abridged) version was published by Pyramid Books (top left) in 1952, 17 years after the original 1935 Liveright hardcover edition. In the early 1970s Liveright (top right), Pocket Books (bottom left), and Tandem (British) all brought out unabridged paper editions. The Indian on the cover of the Liveright edition is Sitting Bull, a Sioux chief who died in 1890. The "major motion picture" announced on the cover of the Pocket Book edition (1972) had not appeared by the spring of 1977.*

A PROUD APACHE

FIVE YEARS after Juanito Razon's death Edwin Corle began work on a fictional account of his life. Corle first wrote a short story which he meant to include in *Mojave,* his collection of stories about the California desert. He soon found, however, that the Fig Tree John material was too expansive to be conveniently incorporated into a short story, so he published *Mojave* without the story and later expanded the story into a full-length novel. That novel, published in 1935, would have either amused or angered Juanito Razon. It is just as well that he did not live to see what was made of his life, for the plot of Corle's novel would have sounded strange indeed to him:

In 1906 Agocho, an Apache Indian in his mid-forties, decides to make a journey away from his reservation in central Arizona. He takes with him Kai-a, the youngest of his three wives, who is six months pregnant. They travel west, with no particular aim in mind. When they get to Yuma, on the Arizona-California border, they hear from local Indians about how the white man had angered the Colorado River by diverting part of it through a canal designed to take water to their farms in the desert. The river had gotten angry and had taken revenge by flooding the canal and filling up a basin in the heart of the desert with foul-tasting salt water. Agocho decides he wants to see this vast inland sea, this symbol of the river spirit's angry rejection of the white man's tampering with nature. With his wife he crosses the river and strikes out across the desert to find the sea.

When he arrives he is so impressed with the beauty of the spot that he decides to stay on for awhile — at least until Kai-a's baby is born. He finds a spring near the banks of the sea and sets up camp. Kai-a plants six fig tree sprays that an Indian woman had given her in Yuma and, watered by the spring, these soon take root and grow. Three months later the baby is born, and the delighted Agocho names him N'Chai Chidn. Things are going so well that he decides to stay on a little longer at the spring.

Three years later Agocho is still living near the spring. One day, when he is in Mecca trading some of his wife's baskets for ammunition for his rifle, two white gangsters running from a posse wander into Agocho's camp. They steal Agocho's two remaining horses. When Kai-a tries to stop them, they knock her unconscious. Then one of the gangsters rapes her and sets Agocho's hut, with her in it, on fire. When Agocho returns several hours later he finds the charred remains of his home and his wife. Intent on revenge, he leaves food for his bewildered three-year-old son and sets out on the track of the gangsters. He catches up with them just as they board a freight train, but he is seconds too late, and they escape. Agocho decides that he must stay on at the Salton Sea if he is ever to get his revenge against these terrible white men. He stays there, solitarily raising his son in the old Apache ways.

A dozen years later Agocho and N'Chai Chidn are still there. The fig trees are now producing. Agocho is known as Fig Tree John by the white people whose date farms are coming ever closer to his camp. N'Chai Chidn is fast approaching manhood. Although Agocho is determined to raise his son as an Apache, N'Chai Chidn is increasingly fascinated by the white men and their ways. Finally, without his father's permission, N'Chai Chidn gets a job on one of the date ranches and adopts a new name: Johnny Mack. The "Johnny" is from his father, the "Mack" is adopted from a neighboring white date rancher's name. Johnny Mack eventually falls in love with Maria, a lovely young Mexican servant-girl from a nearby ranch, and decides that he wants to buy a Ford car and marry Maria. When Agocho learns of all this he is furious, but his son will not be dissuaded. When Johnny builds a little house at his father's camp, and then brings his bride back to live in it with him, Agocho decides that this is his god-given chance to get revenge. One day when his son is away he brutally beats and rapes Maria, whom he thinks of as a white woman.

Johnny Mack does nothing about this incident, for his father's will is stronger than his, but six months later, when Agocho tries to murder Maria, Johnny comes to his wife's assistance and rescues her. She recovers, but moves away to a nearby town, leaving both Johnny Mack and Agocho. Later, when she discovers that she is pregnant with Johnny's child, she writes to him and asks him to join her in town. The delighted Johnny prepares to move, but Agocho, infuriated that his son is leaving, attacks Johnny's Ford with his ax. The final showdown has come, and in the resulting scuffle Johnny murders his father with the ax.

After burying his father in the old Apache way, Johnny loads up the car and drives off to join his wife for a new life in town. Johnny has become, in essence, a white man.

This simple plot summary is, of course, an inadequate summary of a novel which is far richer. The characters in Edwin Corle's *Fig Tree John* are far more complex and convincing than they can appear in so brief a summary. Indeed, the novel has been highly praised by critics. One recent critic thinks it ranks with the best novels written by "Hemingway and Lewis and Dreiser and Steinbeck."[1] Another calls it "one of our greatest novels about the predicament of the American Indian."[2] Still another calls it "the finest novel about an Indian that has yet been written."[3] Those who praise the novel often do so in part because it presents so convincing, so perceptive, and so objective a portrait of its main character.

On the other hand, those few readers who have expressed in print serious dissatisfaction with the novel have criticized it because it is not true, because it presents, for the most part, lies about its main character. These are the readers who knew the "real" Fig Tree John, Juanito Razon, the old Indian who served as the model for Corle's main character. The most outspoken of these critics was Nina Paul Shumway, who referred to Corle's novel as a "libelous fabrication"[4] and who was so annoyed with it that she with a friend, Leland Yost, wrote an article to present the "true" picture of the old Indian. This article, which appeared in *Desert Magazine* five years after the novel was published, is worth reprinting here in full. It has little direct commentary on Corle's novel, but it is the most complete account of Juanito Razon's life published to date, and it will serve as a convenient summary of what was readily known about the real Fig Tree John at the time Corle was writing. Although subsequent research shows that the Shumway and Yost article contains several inaccuracies and misjudgments, it is a strong and sympathetic sketch and provides a useful contrast with the plot summary of the novel. Shumway and Yost, two Coachella Valley residents who remembered well the old Cahuilla Indian who had once made frequent calls at their ranch houses, did not like the title given to their article by the editors of *Desert Magazine,* for it is certain the old man's gun would have been loaded some of the time, at least when he went hunting in the hills. The article is quoted, however, as it originally appeared in 1941:

Fig Tree John's Gun was Never Loaded

It was the 25th of December but the California sun beamed ardently on the crowd that was beginning to gather around the long barbecue tables in the little desert town of Coachella. Ungreased wheels screeching, a buggy crawled down the dusty street and stopped under a lacy avalanche of pepper-tree branches where a dozen or more other Indian rigs and saddle-ponies were tied in the shade. A man climbed down and, followed by an ample brown woman in full-skirted calico, started toward the barbecue tables. Before the pair had taken a score of steps, cameras were out in the crowd. Someone shouted:

"Hi, Fig Tree, stand still. I want to take your picture." The man halted and stood there in the blaze of desert sunlight, a grotesque yet oddly dignified figure. His short muscular body was clothed in a frayed blue army uniform whose brass buttons glittered. On his head, almost resting on his ears was a tall black silk "topper," a bit rusty and scuffed by time and use, but still impressive. Under its brim shrewd black eyes looked out through slits in a strong dark mask of bone and skin carved by age as boulders are carved by erosion. He did not lean on the cane he carried. It was merely for effect — part of the costume he always wore for gala occasions like this Christmas celebration of 1910.

That is how many of us who were Coachella valley pioneers best remember Fig Tree John. It is a sort of landmark in our memories. We would like to keep it, as we try to keep our other landmarks, from being defaced by vandals. We would like to replace in popular thought the false picture of a vile and degenerate savage that fiction has painted, the dirty daub of rumor, with a recognizable likeness of Fig Tree John — chief of the Agua Dulce (Sweet Water) clan of Cahuilla Indians — whose name and colorful personality interwoven with the earliest history of this valley, our Pioneer society is to commemorate with a boulder bearing an inscribed tablet.

Others among his race, primitive inhabitants of the Coachella section of the Colorado desert, were outstanding men of their type. Fig Tree belonged to no type. He was an individualist. They were Indians. He was Fig Tree John.

According to his son, Johnny Mack, Fig Tree John was in his 136th year and still fairly sound of mind and body when an attack of flu took him off on April 11, 1927. No one who had seen him could doubt this reckoning. His feet, more than his face, showed how far he had come over the primitive trail of time. Horny and splayed like an ancient eagle's they had lost almost the last trace of human semblance. Usually they were bare, though he could crowd them into shoes if the occasion were important enough. Like many of the older Cahuillas he sometimes wore the native sandals — mere footpads of matted yucca fibre an inch or more thick, held on by thongs. When traveling without his wife he rode horseback, until about 1910. After that he used the buggy which apparently never knew the benefit of axle-grease.

His real name was *Juanita Razón*. Chester A. Pinkham, who came to the valley in 1891, often wrote letters for him. Mr. Pinkham frequently camped by the spring on Fig Tree's ranchería, and came to know him as well as a white man could. He explained to Fig Tree that Juanita was the feminine of Juanito, little John (or as he would say, Johnny). It made no difference. Fig Tree insisted that the name be signed Juanita and care be taken that the accent mark be placed over the last syllable of Razón.

His nickname came from the planting of Black Mission figs around the spring beside which he lived in a wattled jacal — a hut of arrow weed and mud, a primitive type of dwelling he never gave up. The trees were mature when the first white settlers came to the valley. The cuttings must have been brought from one of the missions, probably when Juanita attended one of the great Indian gatherings to which all the peaceful tribes, designated after the coming of the padres as Mission Indians, were invited.

It is a mark of his distinction that they were the only fig trees in that part of the country. And, as there were many Juans or Johns, Fig Tree John became a natural identification tag among white men. His spring, well known for its good water, was called by the Cahuillas in their own tongue, *Pal-tookvush-kia-kia-ya-wet* signifying blue water. It became known as "Fig Tree John Spring" and the name was given permanence and some historic importance by its appearing on all early maps and government surveys of the region.

The physical and mental differences that set Fig Tree John apart from his tribesmen gave rise to the stubborn rumor that he was not a Cahuilla but a renegade from Arizona. Those of his race who did not like him, supported this. And a semblance of fact is given it by an incident told by Mr. Pinkham:

A friend of his, Jim Black, seeing Fig Tree for the first time, exclaimed, "Hello, where did that Apache come from?" On being told that Fig Tree was one of the local Cahuillas, Black said, "No, positively no. And I'll prove it." He then saluted Fig Tree in the Apache tongue. Fig Tree, apparently pleased, returned the greeting in the same language. Black said Fig Tree had admitted he came from Arizona many years before. The two men carried on their subsequent conversation in Spanish — the language used by most of the older Cahuillas with white men.

Evidence gathered on the Martinez reservation, headquarters of the Cahuilla Indian agency, discredits the story that Fig Tree was an Apache. On the reservation the Razóns are regarded as an old and well-established Cahuilla family. This is their standing among the clans represented at Santa Rosa, Cahuilla, Palm Springs, Cabezon and Morongo. Fig Tree John died on the Martinez reservation and is buried there in the Catholic cemetery. His wife, a son — Jake, and an only daughter — Mrs. John Roxie, are also buried there. His brother, Billy Razón whose birth date appears on the agency register as 1851, and a nephew namesake of Fig Tree's, Juanito Razón, live on the reservation. There is another nephew, Henry Matthews, who works outside the valley. This is too much family background for a renegade — the lone wolf from another tribe.

August Lomas, an intelligent and well educated Cahuilla whose father was chief of the Martinez clan, said positively, "I know Juanita Razón was a Cahuilla. My people have always known his. He married a woman of the Cabezon clan. He was chief of the Agua Dulce clan. In Cahuilla that is *To-va*. But the real name of the clan is *Tama-ka-ha-chim*."

Johnny Mack, the sole survivor of Fig Tree's immediate family, also used this clan name when talking of his father's origin. He said it meant Indians that in the beginning came from the East. (Could that have been what Fig Tree told Mr. Black — and been misunderstood?)

Johnny says that his father was born at what white men called Fig Tree John spring; that Fig Tree inherited this spring and adjacent lands to the south and west from his father, and that was why he had claimed ownership of them.

The Southern Pacific railroad, either from kindness or diplomacy, waived its claim to the land until Fig Tree John was gone. The era was past when Johnny Mack Razón could hope to inherit the lands of his ancestors. His birthplace is part of the Beach-

Vessey ranch, and Johnny, now 67 years of age, works at the Stratton place on the north shore of Salton sea.

Fig Tree John, perhaps because he was too old when the change came, perhaps because his nature was too primitive and too unyielding, could not accept the fate of his race; he could only fear it. His actions show that after the coming of the settlers he was constantly badgered by fear of being put off the desolate ranchería which had been his home for close to a century.

His defenses were up. Always he tried to impress upon white men the importance of his chieftaincy, the vastness of his domain and his absolute rule over it. His sweeping gesture of dominion would take in the whole vast stretch of waterless wilderness to the south of Rabbit peak in the lower Santa Rosa range, and east to Salton sea.

He resented any infringement of his authority. At one time he put a barb-wire fence around his spring. When Chester Pinkham came he unquestioningly camped outside the enclosure and carried water to his burros. Later, when Pinkham was accompanied by a partner, the partner scorned Fig Tree's tabu. Be darned if any old so-and-so would make him pack water! He'd camp inside, right by the spring.

When they were settled Fig Tree appeared and sternly ordered them outside the fence. The partner refused to move. Fig Tree got his old Winchester and pointed it. The partner reached for his own gun. Fig Tree lowered his, and marched off. But the next time Chester Pinkham came, Fig Tree did not greet him in the customary way as *amigo* — friend, but as *hombre* — man.

If there was nothing to arouse his instinctive fear of the white man's power, Fig Tree John could be kind and hospitable. An instance of this was when he saved the life of another partner of Pinkham's. This youth, "Babe" Smith, rashly undertook against Pinkham's advice to spend the summer in the Carriso section of the desert far to the south of Fig Tree's ranchería. He lost his burros and came crawling half dead into Fig Tree's jacal. The Indian kept him there a week, caring for him until he could travel, then took him horseback into Mecca, the nearest outpost of civilization.

The old days were passing and with them the freedom of the desert's children. The other Cahuillas, by their very docility, were leagued with the whites. It left Fig Tree alone against the world. He set a line of mesquite posts along what he considered his north boundary line and forbade even those of his own race to cross it. His order was backed by a threatening display of his ancient 44-40 model 63 Winchester carbine. The Indian agent, then stationed at San Jacinto, was notified of this outrage. He came down with some Indian police. Fig Tree defied them. He held them off, too, with his antique firearm until a pair of them circled round through the brush and grabbed him from behind. The papers made the most of this uprising. It was evident that old Fig Tree John was a bad Indian.

At various times thereafter he ordered intruders off his ranch-ería, menacing them with the Winchester. This didn't improve his reputation. Eventually the gun proved to be unloaded and minus certain essential shooting-parts. But as long as nobody knew it but Fig Tree, the bluff worked.

By 1914 he had not been seriously molested and felt secure in his stronghold. Once the Paul family loaded up the hayrack and made an overnight camping trip to Salton sea, whose shore lay within the Razón boundary. Fig Tree kept them under his eyes, but beyond warning them that they were on private property, he offered no objection to their visit.

When all were in bed and everything quiet for the night, he and his wife returned to their jacal. By that time this had been moved back to Agua Dulce spring, now on the Daras Cox ranch, where Fig Tree lived after the Colorado broke through and poured into the Salton basin in 1905–7, inundating the homesite at Fig Tree John spring.

At dawn he creaked back in his buggy to stand guard for the day. He brought along a battered straw suitcase containing his uniform and top hat in which he offered to pose for his photograph, price *un peso*.

Where he got this historic outfit is a mystery. Hearsay has it that the uniform was issued to him by the government when he acted as a scout for General Fremont. There seems to be no sound basis for this story. His name is not listed with those of U.S. scouts. Yet Johnny Mack insists that his father acted as a scout for Fremont. It is reasonable to conclude that in an unofficial capacity Fig Tree guided a detachment of soldiers across the badlands at the extreme lower end of the Santa Rosas in the region of 17 Palms.

Johnny does not claim that the uniform was a relic of his father's service. He doesn't know just how either that or the hat was acquired. But he says that as he remembers it, once when he was a very little boy his father took him to Los Angeles to some kind of Indian meeting. He thinks that there somebody gave Fig Tree the outfit.

Anyway it was a fine thing to have when the cameras came along. And Fig Tree soon learned to put a price on posing in it. He had a talent for making money, rare even in the educated

Cahuilla. When the original Southern Pacific tracks were submerged by the outbreak of the Colorado river that formed the present Salton sea, Fig Tree John hired a crew of Indians to salvage the ties that washed ashore. There was a ready market for them among incoming settlers who needed fenceposts. The railroad again respected Fig Tree's "rights" and the old chief did a thriving business as long as the ties lasted.

Trading was another way in which he showed his commercial instinct, especially horse trading. In early days he always managed to keep a herd of lean ponies on his ranchería. And he made a good thing out of swapping them. He liked to spend two or three days dickering, getting all the fun and profit that could be squeezed out of a deal.

His love of barter was carried even into the kitchens of friendly housewives in the Oasis district — the agricultural settlement nearest his ranchería — and the housewives very seldom came out ahead. When Mrs. Yost received a watermelon from Fig Tree's patch, she gave, by request, a bag of sugar, or a pound of coffee. Yet he would always present his offering with the ceremonious air of making a gift. Then he would sit around letting his generosity soak in before he indicated what he would be pleased to accept in return.

When he had nothing to exchange, he tried just asking for what he wanted. It often worked. He made a habit of calling about once a week on various housewives and frankly stating what food he craved. Usually he got it. There was one startling exception. He made his regular call at a certain home and found nobody around but the small boy of the family — a great friend of Fig Tree's. Fig Tree asked where the señora was, and the youngster took the old chief by the hand and led him upstairs and into the room where the lady was in her bath. For once Fig Tree left without asking for anything.

Despite his independence, Fig Tree in his later years depended more and more on the generosity of his white neighbors for his food supply. With increasing age, and the scarcity of wild game, his trips into the Santa Rosas on hunting and foraging trips became less frequent. The seeds and nuts and roots of the aboriginal diet were hard to gather and prepare, and were not nearly so tasty or easy on the gums as corned beef and canned peaches — his favorite dainties.

His visits to the store at Mecca were important occasions. They were always made on a week-day when the clerks would have plenty of time to give him. Mrs. Razón was permitted to purchase cloth and trinkets, but Fig Tree bought the provisions. With great deliberation he selected one article at a time and paid for it before going on to the next. At the end he never forgot to ask for the *pilón* — the gift that among the Mexicans takes the place of our cash discount.

Fig Tree paid cash — or its equivalent. There are reliable people who say that he sometimes paid "Gene" Hill, the pioneer merchant at Mecca, with raw gold. Mr. Hill is dead and there is no way to prove the report, which has been twisted into all sorts of shapes from the usual lost mine to the myth about a prospector murdered for his gold.

If Fig Tree ever had raw gold in his possession, the chances are he received it in payment for a pony or provisions either from a prospector or an Indian from the Colorado river country where gold was fairly plentiful in early days. But that is only a guess.

Many people have asked for the truth about Fig Tree John. The best we can do is to winnow out what obviously was false or purely speculative and to gather what few authentic facts, incidents, details, memories and pictures remain. The truth about a man is as deep as his soul.

When talking over the drama of early days as it had affected his father, Johnny Mack said, batting at the flies that swarmed over from a nearby corral, "White men are like flies; you fight one off and another comes."

All right, Johnny Mack. Our race deserves that from yours. And what do flies know of the souls of the men they torment — old, old desert men like Fig Tree John standing in the sun?[5]

For readers familiar with the real Fig Tree John, Corle's novel would naturally have seemed an outrageously inaccurate account. It is quite understandable that such readers would refer contemptuously, as Shumway and Yost have done above, to Corle's portrait of Fig Tree John as "the false picture of a vile and degenerate savage that fiction has painted, the dirty daub of rumor." Although the annoyance of such readers is essentially irrelevant to literary criticism, it does alert us to several questions which are of legitimate relevance to a literary evaluation of this novel: What did Corle know about Juanito Razon? What changes and additions did he make to transform facts into fiction? Why did he make these conscious alterations of fact? If we can answer these questions, then we shall be better equipped to discover what Corle was trying to say in his novel, *Fig Tree John*.

An awareness of Corle's conception of the real Fig Tree John will throw into sharper relief certain characteristics of his fictional one. And if we can discover, through an analysis of the conscious changes Corle made in the characterization of his main character, what Corle was trying to say or demonstrate in his novel, then we shall better be able to offer an evaluation of how well he said it — how successful his novel is as a demonstration of his themes.

THE FACTS CORLE KNEW

In trying to determine what Edwin Corle knew about Juanito Razon, we have at our disposal only two kinds of information: Corle's own statements about how he wrote the novel, and the incidents in the novel itself, several of which are similar to incidents known to have really happened. For the author's own statements, we are most fortunate to have at our disposal a letter which Corle wrote in 1953, only a few years before his death, to his friend Lawrence Clark Powell. The Ward Ritchie Press was to bring out a special limited edition of *Fig Tree John,* and Corle wanted Powell to write a foreword. In mid-February the two men got together to talk about the project. Then Powell left with the understanding that Corle would write down some specific information which Powell might draw on for his foreword. Corle's letter came a few days later:

Edwin Corle to Lawrence Clark Powell, *February 18, 1953*

Dear Larry:

It is always exciting to have you here. One of us is more book crazy than the other, but it would take the Supreme Court to decide which and they'd probably get it wrong. You never stay long enough and I always think of a dozen things I meant to say after you have left. I feel a bit remiss for I think I talked too much about myself rather than FIG TREE JOHN.

At any rate, here is some of the FIG TREE background which you may use or discard as you wish.

The scene: I first saw the Salton Sea in 1920 from a Pullman car on the Southern Pacific's "Sunset Limited." The bleakness and mystery of the place stayed with me. In 1923 and 1924 I saw the Salton Sea from the main highway that runs along its southwestern fringe from Mecca to Westmoreland. In making a number of trips back and forth between Hollywood and El Centro I was attracted by an Auto Club of So. Cal. sign pointing off the road. The sign read "Fig Tree John" and probably indicated "water" at "one mile" or less. The odd name struck me and I was curious to know more about it. I heard then that Fig Tree was an Indian.

The development: In 1933 while writing a series of short stories set in the California desert regions I decided to include one story on Fig Tree John and went about finding out who and what he was. The first draft of the story was clumsy and seemed to have no end. When I had about 16 or more stories ready to make into a book to be called MOJAVE, I dropped the Fig Tree John material as too cumbersome and not sufficiently developed. The book MOJAVE was published in 1934.

The novel: After trying the Fig Tree John material again I found that it could not be disciplined into the short story form. The reason was that the subject had developed in characterization and had spun itself out over a period of years. Obviously it would lend itself to a novel.

The writing: I had learned that Fig Tree John was a "tough hombre" and not typical of the local Indians. There were rumors that he had been an Apache and had come from Arizona in 1905 or 1906 and had stayed on at the water hole he discovered and never returned to Arizona. This may have been mere rumor, but it added fuel to my story. Using this as a point of departure I made my character a White Mountain Apache from the White River country of central Arizona. These are the wild and warlike Apaches, more or less typical of the Athapascan stock. My theme or "plot" (a word I resent as [much as] character is plot, and plot per se is mere manipulation and thereby false) was the result of Fig Tree's running into white civilization. The irresistible body (white civilization) hit the immovable object (Apache civilization) and something had to happen. The result meant the end of the Indian; in this case the race symbolized by Fig Tree himself. The next generation "goes white," and the son of Johnny Mack and Maria the Mexican girl will be entirely conditioned by white civilization. The orthodox Indian will die out. Fig

Tree represents the violent end of the non-conformist. He will never quit; he has to be killed. It's all or nothing, win or lose, victory or death with him.

Research: For the Apache culture I read widely in the library of the Southwest Museum. All I needed was there and I had to look no further. For the life and blood contact I went to Arizona and observed Apaches in the White River area. I also did some research about the town of Yuma and the Indians who lived there in 1906; learned the story of the runaway river when the Colorado created the Salton Sea; lived for a few days with rancher Edward P. Carr whose land was next to that claimed by Fig Tree. Carr was a man of erudition and he told me he was certain that Fig Tree was an Apache. He also told me the story of Johnny Mack and how he grew up and "went white" much to Fig Tree's disgust; also how Johnny took a wife and that Fig Tree considered the wife his as much as his son's, and that she was simply to be used by them both (Apaches were polygamous). Johnny didn't like this but was afraid of Fig Tree and put up with it. So did the girl, presumably. She was either a Mexican or was part Indian-part Mexican.

Fig Tree was dead and Johnny had gone "away" when I did this research. The water hole had been abandoned. This was in 1934 from September into October.

The book was written from October (actually was begun as a book from the original short story on September 3, 1934) and was completed in December (about the 23rd) of 1934.

Liveright's editor was T. R. Smith. He wanted no changes in the text. The book was published in September of 1935.

London Edition: T. Werner Laurie, 1936. Some changes in the text were made to avoid British censorship. Also "gas" was changed to "petrol." Instead of saying "Got any gas?" one Apache buck says to another "I say, old chap, could you spare a bit of petrol?" (This makes a good gag to tell, but it is an exaggeration.) Presumably the second Apache replied, "Surely, old boy, I have plenty, help yourself, ugh." And the first one says, "That's jolly, ugh to you." Audiences like this kind of embroidery.

Quotes: The book had a good press reaction, even from Australia and India. Dr. Hodge's quotation which I forgot to show you reads: "To Edwin Corle who knows the soul of the Indian, with deep appreciation." This is in a book of his called THE HISTORY OF HAWIKUH, which he gave me after reading FIG TREE JOHN.

Well, enough is enough. Out of the above scramble you may find some points that you can use. The limited edition will not go to press before May, so you need not rush anything. 750 words to 1500 will [be] about right. Even a bit over that if you feel there is something to say.[6]

It is clear that Edwin Corle did not know much of the historical information about Juanito Razon which we have uncovered in Part One. For one thing, when Corle "went about finding out who and what" Fig Tree John was, much of the information presented in Part One had not been published or brought to light and so was not known to Edwin Corle: the story of Juanito Razon's real estate controversy with the Southern Pacific Railroad and with the Bureau of Indian Affairs; the story of his possible knowledge of a gold mine in the hills; the story of how he made his living, how he rescued the Grant boys, and how he had many friendships both with local whites and local Indians. For another thing, it appears that Corle relied heavily on the recollections of Coachella Valley residents for his information rather than on written accounts. From Juanito Razon's neighbors Corle learned that the old man, who had died five years earlier, had been a "tough hombre." Carr told him what turned out to have been questionable "facts" about how Fig Tree John had been an Apache, about how he had been annoyed when his son, Johnny Mack, "went white," and about how he had made Johnny share his wife with him. These facts are all rather vague and uncertain, even when we make allowances for Corle's having written down his recollections about how he wrote the novel a good 20 years after the fact. Still, Corle's letter to Lawrence Clark Powell does show that he was interested in the biographical facts of Juanito Razon's life, and that he took pains to find out what he could.

The novel itself is a more reliable indication that Corle took his job as a researcher seriously, for the everyday life of its main character is similar in many ways to that of Juanito Razon. Corle's character is named Agocho, but, as Juanito Razon had been, he is known to whites as Fig Tree

John because of his fig tree orchard. From the descriptions in the novel, Agocho is apparently intended to look very much as Juanito Razon had looked: "He seemed to be shrinking with age. Fig Tree had never been a tall man. . . . His dirty khaki pants looked too large for him, and the muscles of his face were sagging so that there were many lines and wrinkles."[7] Such a description easily could have originated from Corle's having seen one of the many photographs of the original Fig Tree John.

Agocho's general situation is basically similar to that of Juanito Razon. Speaking broken English, he lives away from the reservation lands set aside for his people, near a little spring on the west bank of the Salton Sea, south of the town called Mecca and west of the Southern Pacific Railroad. He lives there with his wife and a son named Johnny Mack. Many of Agocho's actions are similar to Juanito Razon's in this same period. He moves to a new home in 1906, shortly after the formation of the Salton Sea, and remains there for the last 20 years of his life, staunchly defending his right to stay there and live his own kind of life. He considers himself to be the rightful owner of land occupied or claimed by the white farmers around, and he sometimes feels called upon to use force, or threats of force, to establish his own claim. Agocho frightens whites with what turns out to be a harmless rifle: "He's been sittin' out there all day armed to the teeth and lookin' dangerous with an empty rifle."[8] He saves the life of a white man nearly dead from lack of water, then takes him up to Mecca on horseback.

He transacts business at the general store in Mecca and sells his wife's baskets. He asks for (and receives) coffee and sugar from white housewives. He even steals tools and other things from white ranches; to Agocho, as to Juanito Razon, this is not really stealing as much as it is receiving rightful payment for the use of his land: "He became known as a great thief, but he wasn't really a thief, only an arbitrary collector of tithes. . . . The white man was a trespasser and he had no compunction about taking anything useful that these outlanders had brought with them."[9] It is clear, then, that Corle learned a great deal about the real Fig Tree John and that he used at least some of what he learned in his novel.

There is much, however, that Corle did not use, much that he changed, and much that he added. Taken together, these alterations and additions serve to portray a far from accurate picture of Juanito Razon's life and character. Most of the changes which Corle incorporated can be subsumed under one of three major categories. First, whereas Juanito Razon had been a Cahuilla Indian who spent all of his life in the desert, Corle makes Agocho an Apache from central Arizona who migrates to southern California in 1906. Second, whereas Juanito Razon had had many friendly and mutually profitable relationships with white men and women and had adopted many of their ways, Corle gives Agocho a consuming hatred for all white men and for everything that they stand for or are associated with. Third, whereas Juanito Razon had led an essentially ordinary and unexciting life with his wife and family and friends, Corle introduces many plot elements, such as the rape and murder of Agocho's wife by a white gangster.

Corle got the basic notion for Agocho's independence, isolation, and resistance to whites from his real-life model, but in his novel he greatly intensified these aspects and played down or entirely ignored certain others. Corle wanted to make Agocho as memorable as possible by concentrating on and emphasizing some of the most striking elements of his personality, and he wanted to use Agocho to reinforce his theme about the fate of Indians who refuse to adjust to the encroaching presence of the white man in America. Accordingly, Corle made Agocho more fiercely independent and more painfully isolated than was his real-life counterpart. He also made Agocho so completely antagonistic toward white people and their culture that he is doomed, almost from the start, to extinction. Whereas Juanito Razon had died from natural causes at a very old age, Agocho's refusal to adapt to the white man's ways requires that he be murdered at a considerably younger age by a son who is more able than he is to adjust to new times and new ways. Let us consider Corle's three major changes, and the reasons for them, in more detail.

FROM CAHUILLA TO APACHE

There can be no question that Juanito Razon was a local Cahuilla Indian. Although one or two whites who saw him thought that he was an Apache from Arizona, all the solid evidence indicates that he was a local Indian who spent virtually all of his life in the mountains and deserts of southern California. Before we inquire why Corle made his Fig Tree John an Apache, we should ask whether Corle knew that the real Fig Tree John was a Cahuilla. The record is ambiguous. On the one hand, Corle reports in his 1953 letter to Powell that Edward P. Carr, who had been a neighbor of Juanito Razon's, "was a man of erudition and he told me he was certain that Fig Tree was an Apache." On the other hand, he admits in the same letter that "there were rumors that he had been an Apache and had come from Arizona in 1905 or 1906 and had stayed on at the water hole he discovered and never returned to Arizona. This may have been mere rumor, but it added fuel to my story." It is my belief that Corle knew pretty well that such stories were mere rumors.

For one thing, Juanito Razon was *not* an Apache, and it would not have taken much asking around to discover that fact. For another thing, I think it almost certain that Corle was familiar with *California Desert Trails* (1919), J. Smeaton Chase's book about the California desert. Anyone interested enough in this desert region to write a book of stories (*Mojave,* 1934) about it would have known about Chase's book. The index to Chase's book would have led Corle to the following description of a visit to Fig Tree John's camp:

The Indian patriarch of these parts is old Juan Razon, or, as he is better known, "Figtree John." In former times he lived, far from whites and other Indians, at a spot a few miles to the south. It is to be known by a few fig trees and is marked on Government maps as Figtree John Springs. When the Salton Sea submerged his little estate he moved to another spot, called Agua Dulce, on somewhat higher ground. I already had a slight acquaintance with him, and was pleased now to meet him as he was leading his horse to water. When I had surrendered the can of tobacco with which I had come prepared, he invited me to share a watermelon with him at his house. I hastened to agree to this excellent idea. The mellowest *sandía* was brought from his little patch and bisected with a rusty hatchet, and we sat in shade of the *ramada* and chatted while the cooling hemispheres rapidly melted away. To my regret, Mrs. John was coy and would not join us, nor would a huge girl who gloomily watched the melon's effacement through peepholes in the brush partition.

From a chummy, almost fraternal, tone, John became impressive. An old satchel was produced, and proved to contain archives that revealed my friend in higher rôles. First was a photograph, tenderly wrapped, of himself *en cavalier,* wearing a police uniform the feature of which, apart from a certain roominess of fit, was its double rows of gleaming buttons. The severity of a stovepipe hat gave effect to an attitude of martial rigidity which he had thought proper on the occasion of being "taken." A possible defect of topheaviness was offset by bare feet which corrected any impression of overdress. The steed, appropriate for a desert chieftain, was a minute donkey, whose dramatically pointed ears betokened a deep sense of responsibility.

Next an aged document was perilously unfolded and spread before me. In clerkly hand and formal phrase it set forth that Cabezon, the last great chief of the Cahuillas, did thereby name and appoint Juanito (= Johnny, or Little John) Razon to be *capitan* of the Agua Dulce Tuba village, and to exercise authority in the name, place, and stead of said Chief Cabezon; and called upon his people to render respect and obedience to said Johnny in all said Johnny's lawful commands: etc., etc.: "given under my hand this so-and-so," and signed with a cross in presence of a witness. Then came some ragged maps, apparently rough drafts of surveyors. These, he held, made him owner of all the territory shown, running from the last low ridge of the Santa Rosas (the ridge was named Hiawat on the map, evidently an Indian word, though John could not translate it into Spanish) as far as Conejo Prieto or Black Rabbit Peak. No wonder he eyed me closely while these valuable papers were in my grasp.

Before I left I bought of him a *mecate* or rope of plaited horse-hair, of his own making. The price to others would have been four dollars, he said, but on grounds of friendship I should have it for half the sum. This statement warned me that the article was not worth the price he asked me for it, but I was glad to carry away this souvenir of the dusky lord of Conejo Prieto. There is a legend, the truth of which I may some day put to the proof, that the rattlesnake will not cross a rope of this sort. Many cowboys and others are convinced that this is a fact, and John also affirmed it stoutly. . . .

When I suggested a picture it was made plain to me that the great do not receive but confer a favor in being photographed. John demanded a round sum, which in this case seemed not to be modified on the score of friendship. When that was arranged he took the position and expression of one who bears intense pain with determination. Then the great girl would be taken with her pet goat. No need for any formula of "Look pleasant, please," with smiling Juana. When I asked how I should address her in sending copies of the picture, she sedately gave her name as Mrs. So-and-so, Post-office box so-and-so, at Mecca; thoroughly up in the ways of the world. No doubt her children will be little Bills and Bobs, Sadies and "Soosies," with chewing-gum and all modern improvements.

An hour's easy ride brought me to my camping place for the night at Figtree John Springs, no longer obliterated by the flood. The water is good though tepid, and a few small palms and a cottonwood or two make the spot attractive. The margin of the lake is now half a mile away. I walked over to it, and found an uninviting beach of slimy mud, the surface baked by the sun into large curving flakes like potsherds. . . .

I turned now northwesterly, following the route taken (as I think likely) by Anza and his fellow explorers. To my right rose an isolated dark mass called Coyote Mountain, which Figtree John claims as his birthplace. One could hardly imagine a more unattractive place to call one's native spot; yet no, I remember the slums of man's cities.[10]

Chase's book undoubtedly was the source for several of the details which appear in Corle's novel: the location of a home "far from whites and other Indians"; the shy wife who retires to the hut when a strange white man arrives; Fig Tree John's claim to personal ownership of a large tract of land; the expected gift of tobacco from a white visitor; the clothes too big for the small man; the homemade horsehair rope; perhaps even the hatchet or ax. It also may have given Corle the idea for having the son "Johnny" become essentially a white man: Chase had spoken of how the Razons' children "will be little Bills and Bobs, Sadies and 'Soosies,' with chewing-gum and all modern improvements." Since it seems certain that Corle was familiar with Chase's book, he would have known that before the Salton Sea rose in 1905–07, Juanito Razon had lived, not far to the east, but merely "a few miles to the south" at another spring. He also would have known that Fig Tree John was born, not in central Arizona, but at Coyote Mountain, only 20 miles to the west of the Salton Sea.

Additional evidence of Corle's knowledge that Fig Tree John was not an Apache comes from another source. Corle said in his letter to Powell that he had written a short story about Fig Tree John for inclusion in *Mojave*, his book of desert stories. He did not include that story in *Mojave*, however, and the story is no longer in existence. (Corle apparently destroyed the original short story, for a 1974 search through his papers by his widow, Mrs. Jean Corle, revealed no trace of it.) Corle did, however, include a story called "Bank Holiday" in the completed volume, and in that story there is a brief reference to Fig Tree John. "Bank Holiday" takes place at the start of the Depression. Four Indians who know nothing about the Depression are wondering why the First National Bank of Coachella is closed. They decide to wait until another Indian, John Whitewater, comes along. John will be able to explain this disruption in the white man's economic system, because "John Whitewater had been a friend of old Fig Tree John, and Fig Tree John had been the wisest Indian in the methods of the white men in all the Colorado Desert. Fig Tree John was reputed to have been one of Frémont's scouts, and to have killed five men. Nobody knew if that were true, and nobody cared any more because old Fig Tree was dead. But his wisdom lived after him in the person of John Whitewater." Later, when John Whitewater does give a kind of explanation, the other Indians accept it: "John Whitewater had been the friend of Fig Tree John, and that was authority enough."[11]

This allusion to Fig Tree John is interesting both because it represents Corle's early conception of Fig Tree John's character, and also because it comes closer to describing the real Fig Tree John than does the novel version written a year later. It is important to note not only that this allusion makes no reference to Fig Tree John's being an Apache, but also that it suggests that he may have been a scout for John Charles Frémont, the colorful California explorer and military officer. For Fig Tree John to have been a scout for Frémont, he would have had to be living in the southern California desert in 1849 when Frémont made the only one of his expeditions which would have taken him anywhere near the Salton Sea area. And if Fig Tree John were there then, he could scarcely, as in the novel, have been an Apache migrating for the first time in 1906. It seems clear, then, that Corle knew well enough that Fig Tree John was a Cahuilla Indian. His making him an Apache in the novel was a conscious decision — a conscious altering of fact for the sake of fiction.

The most obvious reason for changing Fig Tree John from a Cahuilla to an Apache, of course, is that hardly anyone outside of southern California has ever heard of the Cahuilla Indians, whereas virtually everyone knows of the Apaches. The very name "Apache" connotes a number of the qualities Corle wanted his character to possess: independence, toughness, cruelty, vengefulness. As Corle himself said in his 1953 letter to Powell, "I made my character a White Mountain Apache from the White River country of central Arizona. These are the wild and warlike Apaches." The reason for the change, however, goes far deeper than merely to make Agocho "wild and warlike."

Because Agocho is a lone Apache far from his homeland, he is almost totally isolated. Juanito Razon, it is true, had made his camp a little further south than had most of the other Cahuillas, but he had lived on land that had been occupied by his clan for years. Also, he had many contacts with other Cahuillas — friends, relatives, tribesmen. Corle apparently knew something of the real Fig Tree John's contacts with other Indians, for in the "Bank Holiday" allusion,

John Whitewater was said to have been his good friend, and the other four Indians all greatly respected his wisdom. All of this is excluded from the novel. Agocho never sees another Apache in the story except his wife, who is murdered early in the story, and his son, who, since he has "gone white," is not really an Apache any more by the end of the novel. Agocho's alienation is accentuated even more when he is murdered by his own son. There are other Indians around the Salton Sea, but in 20 years Agocho never gets to know them. Even when he does encounter them, he considers them to be "obviously inferior to Apaches,"[12] and arrogantly holds them in contempt. While this isolation may seem to increase our sympathy for Agocho, we should recall that the isolation is almost entirely self-imposed. No one forces Agocho to come to California, no one forces him to stay, and no one forces him to cut himself off from local Indians. I suspect that for Corle the isolation of his main character was intended primarily, not to make him more sympathetic, but to concentrate the focus of the novel, and to emphasize Agocho's fierce independence and pride.

From one point of view Agocho's being an Apache away from home serves to decrease our sympathy for him, because his claim to "his" land is no more legitimate than that of the white men he hates. Corle does not permit his readers to stand aghast in righteous indignation that this poor Indian is deprived of his land. This land is not Agocho's. He is just a squatter. He is one of the last to lay claim to the desert regions, not one of the first. When Agocho angrily claims the land around him "by right of personal conquest,"[13] we can only smile because he has conquered nothing. He just walked in and built a hut beside a spring and planted some trees. When the indignant Agocho finds it beyond his comprehension that a "white intruder"[14] can "take something to which he has no right or privilege whatever, and immediately convince himself that it is his, has always been his, and will forever be his,"[15] we smile again because this is precisely what Agocho has done. Juanito Razon, on the other hand, had had a right to be angry when white men encroached on his land, for he was living on land which he and his family had long lived on, and which they had official right to live on. At one point in Corle's novel, when Agocho belligerently rides up to a white neighbor and demands that he leave, the neighbor asks, "What makes you think this is your property? Have you got a title?"[16] Agocho can only stand silent, for of course he has none. Chase tells us that Juanito Razon, on the other hand, had had a duly authorized paper from old Chief Cabazon making him a *capitan* and giving him authority over a wide expanse of land. He also had received a letter from the Special Commissioner to the Indians of California telling him that he had every right to stay on his land, and even to expand his holdings.[17] If Corle had made Agocho an Apache on his own land, or a Cahuilla on his own land, we would have sympathized when white men came and tried to squeeze him in, or squeeze him out. As an Apache on lands which his tribe never claimed, however, Agocho has no more right to our sympathy than the white men have.

This brings us to what I call the "transplant theme" in *Fig Tree John*. Agocho, as an Apache from Arizona, comes to the California desert and transplants himself, as he transplants his wife, and as she transplants fig trees. Similarly, white ranchers transplant Deglet Noor date palms from Morocco and effectively "transplant" or divert part of a river. This theme of transplanting something or some person to a foreign setting is too pervasive to have been accidental, and surely it accounts in part for Corle's wanting Agocho to be a non-California Indian in California. Most of these transplants are more or less successful and productive. The river is successfully diverted through the canal to make the desert bloom. The date farms flourish. The fig trees take root quickly and produce excellent fruit. Kai-a, Agocho's wife, brings forth her own fruit (Johnny) in the new land, and Johnny successfully adapts himself to his environment.

Only Agocho does not flourish. While everything around him — all new life to the desert — is fertile and productive, Agocho is withering and sterile. It is interesting to note in this regard that Agocho had impregnated Kai-a back in Apache country, but seems unable to do so again in the new land. Nor is it an accident that Agocho later turns out to be impotent in his second sexual encounter with Maria, his son's wife, for Agocho's inability to produce new life in his new setting is part of Corle's point in the novel. Agocho is something of a dinosaur. He is doomed to extinction because he cannot adapt to new surroundings and changing ways. This is the central and controlling theme of Corle's *Fig Tree John:* to survive and be productive in the new world, people must adapt to changed conditions and surroundings, or they must die out to make room for those, more fit, who can adapt. Agocho's being an Apache, then, is absolutely essential in Corle's story; the change from local Cahuilla to transplanted Apache was a carefully considered contribution to the Darwinian theme of the novel.

This change, however, introduced a serious problem for Corle, one which he was able to solve with only partial success. I am referring to the problem of motivating Agocho's migration from his Arizona homeland to California in 1906. Why would an Apache leave two of his wives and all of his friends on the Apache reservation and travel on horseback some 500 miles across desolate range, river, and desert, with a wife who is six months pregnant? Corle is noticeably vague about explaining the purpose or reason for that trip. We are told that Apaches are "a nomadic tribe" and that on this trip Agocho is "traveling toward the setting sun each day,"[18] but apparently he has no definite destination. When he gets to Yuma on the Arizona-California border he has a conversation with two local Indians (a Yuma and a Yavapai): "Neither of the Indians asked Agocho why he was traveling, why he had left his own country, where he was going, or how long he intended to stay."[19] And since Agocho does not volunteer any of this information, we never do find out. Once he does get to Yuma and finds out about how the

"River Spirit" had gotten revenge on the white men, then he is motivated to go see it for himself because of his hatred of white men and his desire to see proof of their defeat. But none of this is very convincing. In 1906 Juanito Razon also had moved to a new home beside the Salton Sea, but his motivation for doing so was convincing and unambiguous. He *had* to move when the rising waters inundated his old home a few miles to the south. Corle, of course, could not motivate his Apache from Arizona to move to *escape* the rising flood waters of the Salton Sea, since Agocho leaves Arizona after the flood is over and goes to *see* the effects of the flood. To motivate Agocho's unconvincing desire to make the move from Arizona, Corle falls back on a vague wanderlust on Agocho's part and on his only partially explained hatred of the white man.

FROM EASY ADAPTATION TO FIERCE RESISTANCE

Agocho's hatred of and resistance to all men and things white was Corle's second major change in his story of the life and doings of Fig Tree John. Juanito Razon had been socially, economically, and spiritually interactive with his white neighbors. He was friendly with most of his neighbors, traded with them, helped them, served as their guide, usually welcomed them to his camp, and went to their holiday celebrations. He learned how to earn money to buy things he needed in the white man's store. He gathered gold in the hills, sold railroad ties salvaged after the Salton Sea receded, sold some of the fruit he raised, and posed for photographs. He was a Christian, attended the little Catholic church on the reservation, and was buried in the Catholic cemetery when he died. White men were to be found within his own family. His sister married a Mormon and, later, Juanito Razon visited his half-white nephew frequently. He sent one of his sons to a white man's boarding school. He dressed like a white man, his favorite outfit consisting of an army coat and silk top hat. He even ate like a white man, enjoying coffee and canned peaches, this last apparently his favorite treat. Juanito Razon, then, was very much part of, and influenced by, the white culture which surrounded him. To be sure, he stood up for his rights and resented unlawful or disrespectful encroachment on his land, but, for the most part, he was friendly to white people.

Corle changed all this. Agocho steadfastly refuses almost all contact with whites. He does not welcome them to his camp, does not go to their holiday celebrations, does not let his son go to their schools, and certainly does not go to their church. From them he *needs* only shells for his rifle; from them he *wants* only tobacco, whiskey, and to be left alone. Unlike his real-life counterpart, he does not deal with white men in gold, in railroad ties, or in horses. He raises figs to eat, not, as Juanito Razon had done, to sell at white markets in Los Angeles. His wife makes baskets, but she makes them out of boredom, not, as Juanito Razon's wife had done, out of a need or desire for money; Agocho later trades his wife's baskets for goods only as an afterthought. He gets coffee and sugar from a white housewife, not because he wants them or has any use for them, but merely because they are something to demand from a race he hates. He wears Indian clothes (except for the khaki pants he wears at the end of his life) and, unlike Juanito Razon, never acquires a wagon.

Corle's changes were not accidental. If Corle, as seems probable, did know Chase's *California Desert Trails,* he would have known about Fig Tree John's fancy white man's dress, about his shrewd selling of a horsehair rope to a white man for two dollars, and about how he charged "a round sum" for having his picture taken. None of this appears in the novel. That Corle was aware of the real Fig Tree John's close relationships with white people seems clear from the short story "Bank Holiday." In the short story Fig Tree John was said to have been a scout for a white military officer; in the novel written a year later he has virtually no contact with whites, certainly not in the capacity of helping white military men. In "Bank Holiday" Fig Tree John was said to be "the wisest Indian in the ways of the white men in all the Colorado Desert"; in the novel this becomes merely "the smartest Indian in the Colorado desert." In the story Fig Tree John was said to be the one Indian who could have explained why the bank was so mysteriously closed; in the novel he has "never heard of a bank." In the short story Fig Tree John was said to have killed "five men"; in the novel this becomes "five white men."[20] These are all small changes, but they serve to demonstrate Corle's conscious shift in the characterization of Fig Tree John from an Indian whose many dealings with whites were mostly quite cordial to one whose few dealings with them are fiercely antagonistic.

Why did Corle want Agocho to be less friendly with, knowledgeable of, and adaptive to whites and their ways than was his prototype? It was partly to show Agocho's independence and isolation, not only from Indians, but also from whites. I think the main reason, however, was to allow Corle to make his main character more primitive. He wanted to show in the novel what happens, not when white society is encountered by an Indian who is partially acculturated, relatively sophisticated, and uncommonly wise in the ways of the white man, but when it is encountered by a primitive Indian who is generally unfamiliar with white ways, able to live by the old ways, and convinced that his own gods are more powerful.

Corle wanted a character for whom the shock of culture contact would be greatest. In his 1953 letter to Powell, Corle said that the subject of his novel was the intersection of widely divergent ways of life: "The irresistible body (white civilization) hit the immovable object (Apache civilization) and something had to happen. . . . The orthodox Indian will die out. Fig Tree represents the violent end of the non-conformist." Corle's Fig Tree John, then, had to be "immovable," "orthodox," and "non-conformist." He had to be one who would fight back not in a "civilized" way by hiring a lawyer and by joining the Mission Indian Federation to protest the iron rule of the Bureau of Indian Affairs, but one who would retaliate with knife and rifle. If Agocho is to be that dinosaur who, because he cannot change and adapt to the new world, is doomed to extinction, then he must be as primitive and as unacculturated as possible.

We must recall, incidentally, that Corle did not really obliterate Juanito Razon's easy adaptability to the ways of the white man; he merely transferred it from Agocho to Agocho's son, Johnny Mack. Johnny Mack in the novel has many of the qualities which Juanito Razon had had in real life: he learns to work at a white man's job; he builds a white man's kind of house; he leans toward the white man's religion; he has friends among his white neighbors; he wears the white man's clothes. What Corle was doing, clearly, was developing his characters so that they would help to demonstrate his theme about the necessity for the American Indian to adapt to the white man's way. Corle could do this most efficiently by developing a contrast between the rigidly anti-white attitudes of the father and the easy adaptability to white ways of the son. For Corle, it was theme which controlled characterization.

FROM EVERYDAY LIFE TO MURDER AND REVENGE

Just as theme controlled characterization, so it also controlled plot. This brings us to the third major category of change which Corle made in adapting fact to fiction. Most of the important events that take place in the novel never happened to Juanito Razon in real life. His wife was not raped and murdered by a white man. He did not take revenge some 20 years later by raping and trying to murder his son's wife. He did not attack his son's car with an ax, and was not in turn attacked and killed with that ax by his son.

Clearly, one of the reasons for the change in plot was to make the story more interesting and readable. Juanito Razon's life was interesting enough, but as near as we can tell it was not sufficiently dramatic or exciting to make a good novel. Murder, rape, a love interest, revenge — all these can be ingredients important to a successful novel, and Corle used them.

Corle's choice of particular plot elements was not controlled by mere sensationalism, however, but by the theme
Corle wanted to present. If Agocho was to be a dinosaur,
a primitive, pre-industrial native, then his basic conflict with
the white man must be not over something as sophisticated
as a boundary line or as esoteric as a theological argument,
but something more basic, more personal, more elemental.
As a result, Corle shows the white man coming into Agocho's
world and violating the two things he holds most dear: first
his wife in an actual rape and murder, and then his son in
a symbolic rape (Johnny yields to a force too strong to resist)
and murder (he ceases being an Apache).

To have the two things most elementally his own thus
taken from him drives Agocho near to madness and inspires
in him a blinding, monomaniacal need for revenge. When
he pursues but is unable to catch up with Joe, the man who
raped and killed Kai-a, he can do no better than duplicate
the crime. After nearly two decades of waiting, Agocho gets
his revenge by raping a "white" woman and then later trying
to kill her. In his distorted perception of his god-given mission, this will atone for the earlier wrong. He seems not to
be aware that his "white" victim is really a Mexican, and
that she was not even remotely connected with Joe's earlier
action. Agocho later similarly misplaces his revenge against
the whites by attacking, not a white man, but an automobile,
and finally his own son. So unreasonable are such actions
that Johnny Mack has no choice but to defend himself, his
property, and his right to do what he must do. The Darwinian
dictum is made manifest. The superior man, the one who
can adapt to the changing world around him, emerges the
victor. Corle, in a rare — and unnecessary — authorial
intrusion, tells us that Agocho should have been aware "that
life might require adjustment on his part," but that such
awareness "was beyond his instinct, beyond his religion, and
beyond his comprehension."[21] This primitive old man, react-
ing to an instinctual perception of a world that no longer
exists and in which he believes the gods personally direct his
activities, does not see that he should adjust his behavior.
As a result he is doomed to carry out a series of actions

which will lead to his own extermination. Those actions, which constitute the plot of Corle's novel, significantly reinforce Corle's theme about the necessity for adaptation.

Theme controlled even the selection of plot details. When Agocho's neighbor, Mr. Paul, visits on the day of Agocho's death, he notices in Agocho's camp the sundial which had earlier been stolen from his wife's cactus garden. This detail was carefully selected by Corle to further exemplify Agocho's denial of "progress." Agocho not only steals this instrument which measures time, he also destroys it by breaking off the dial itself. This is no more than another way for Corle to reinforce the Darwinian theme of his novel. Agocho tries to arrest the passage of time, to deny that things are not what they used to be. To refuse to accept a role in a changed world, to deny the very reality of the sweep of time, is to doom himself to be unfit for a viable life in a changed world. As he destroys the sundial and the advancement of time which it represents, so the advancement of time will destroy him and the inflexible Apache ways he represents. The new world is for those, like Johnny Mack, who can adapt to it.

CORLE AND APACHE ETHNOGRAPHY

It is clear, then, that Edwin Corle put the requirements of good fiction — convincing character, engrossing plot, emphatic theme — before the requirements for full and exact biographical coverage. We should not be surprised to see that he also put the requirements of good fiction before the requirements for full and exact ethnographic coverage.

When Corle made the very important departure from the known facts about Fig Tree John by making him an Apache from central Arizona rather than a Cahuilla Indian native to the desert regions of southern California, he could not use in his novel the information about Indian culture that he discovered on his visits to the Salton Sea area. Juanito Razon, after all, was not an Apache, and neither were any of the other Indians around. The customs and habits of these Indians would have told him nothing about Apache culture.

Instead, Corle had to seek elsewhere for reliable information. As he wrote in his 1953 letter to Powell: "For the
Apache culture I read widely in the library of the Southwest
Museum. All I needed was there and I had to look no further.
For the life and blood contact I went to Arizona and observed
Apaches in the White River area." There is very little that
we can say about what Corle learned by observing Apaches
in Arizona. If he kept a diary or wrote down his impressions,
these are now lost to us. Presumably he observed such things
as how Apaches farmed, what hunting weapons and domestic tools they used, how they behaved with their spouses and
their children, and how they dressed. Whatever he observed
when he was there in the early 1930s, he may have had to
adjust in light of the fact that his fictional character had left
there nearly 30 years earlier and gone to California, never
to return.

We can be a little more confident when we try to determine what Corle may have read about Apaches in the Southwest Museum in Los Angeles, for in the early 1930s the
published information about Apache Indians was not yet
of great volume. It is certain that Corle read and used Reagan's monograph entitled *Notes on the Indians of the Fort
Apache Region*.[22] Basing my conclusions on certain specific
parallels between details in *Fig Tree John* and details in
other works on Apaches which would have been available
to Corle at this time, I believe that Corle probably also had
looked at the following books and monographs at the Southwest Museum library: Goddard's *Myths and Tales from the
White Mountain Apache*;[23] Cremony's *Life Among the
Apaches*;[24] Bourke's *On the Border with Crook*[25] and *Medicine-Men of the Apache*;[26] and Hodge's *Handbook of American Indians*.[27] These publications afford us a useful basis
for comparison with what we read in Corle's novel about
Apache customs: what Apaches eat, how they cook, how
they build their houses, what their ceremonies are like, what
supreme beings they worship, how they bury their dead, what
their attitudes toward white people are, and so on. I shall
not try to evaluate these sources as to the reliability of the
information they present about Apaches, any more than to

say that, while subsequent researchers have corrected some of the information they record about Apaches, they were all considered reliable in their own day and are still read today for the firsthand information they present about Apache life before 1930. The important point here is that Corle read them, or read in them, and that he incorporated some of the information they contained, directly or with certain changes, into his novel.

Before considering the ways in which Corle made use of these ethnographic materials, we should briefly consider certain general principles which seem to have guided him in his selection and treatment of Apache background information. For one thing, as a novelist rather than an ethnographer, Corle had to simplify complex materials. Rather than go into great detail about the complex mythology of the Apaches, for example, Corle simply highlighted it by mentioning three figures: the virgin Goddess Ste-na-tlih-a and her two sons, Na-yen-ez-gan-i (the War God) and Tu-ba-dzis-chi-ni (the Water God). Rather than try to go into great detail about how the Apache puberty ceremony is conducted, Corle highlighted only a few elements and conveniently had Agocho forget or be ignorant of the rest. In simplifying, Corle had to keep in mind not only that too much ethnographic detail would interfere with the forward movement of his story, but also that his audience would have neither the training nor the interest to digest the complex and sometimes contradictory mass of information he could have used.

What ethnographic material he did use he had to make easily comprehensible and plausible to a white audience. He phoneticized the spelling of Ests'unnadlehi to the simpler Ste-na-tlih-a, and made her not the mythological figure she was in his source,[28] but a "goddess." Most white readers could more easily fit a goddess into their theological frame of reference than a mythological figure. When whites think of legendary or mythological figures they probably think of Paul Bunyan and King Arthur. By simplifying the mythological figure into a goddess, Corle assured his audience that Ste-na-tlih-a was a serious figure in the Apache religious system, and not just a character in a children's story.

In addition to simplifying much of the ethnographic material available to him, Corle also found that he had to omit much of it. One reason for this is that, whereas the writers of his ethnographic sources were for the most part writing about a *people* and their way of life, Corle was writing about a *person* and his way of life. As a result, we find that Corle omits all mention of certain Apache customs and rites which would not contribute to the development of his characters. We seek in vain in the novel for information about the Apaches' kinship system, their agricultural methods and social dances, their methods of warfare and hunting, their curing ceremonies and sweat lodges. The reason for Corle's omitting these is partly that most of them involve communal interaction with other tribal members, while Agocho is isolated miles away from the rest of his tribe. It is also, in part, merely that they would have contributed little to the story of Agocho and his life near the Salton Sea.

Corle's decision whether to use intact, to simplify, or to omit entirely a given piece of ethnographic data was almost always based on his answer to the question, "What good will it do my novel?" We recall that Corle said in his 1953 letter to Powell that, "For the Apache culture I read widely in the library of the Southwest Museum. All I needed was there." It is important to note that Corle said, "all I needed," not "all that is known."

A RING OF AUTHENTICITY

Because usefulness controlled all, it is important to consider how Corle did use ethnographic material in *Fig Tree John*. He used it, we shall find, in three primary ways: first, to provide a core of authenticity for his novel; second, to provide a fixed point of departure from which to measure the extent of Johnny Mack's cultural change from Apache ways to white ways; and, third, to provide an explanation for certain of Agocho's otherwise inexplicable actions and attitudes.

Corle provided a ring of authenticity to his work by incorporating details which make the novel more believable and which help to make the characters in it more convincing as Indians. An example is Corle's use of Apache names and Apache language. His main character's name, he tells us, is Agocho Koh Tli-chu, which means Red Fire Bird. Agocho's wife is named Bi-Tli-Kai Nalin, which means White Deer's Daughter, and his son is named N'Chai Chidn, which means Great Spirits. Agocho's best friend back on the reservation is called Long Ears, an authentic Apache name which Corle had probably read in one of the Bourke books.[29]

Agocho's reluctance to tell white people his real name ("They certainly never would learn his real name. He'd see to that."[30]) might also stem from Bourke, although Cremony is a more likely source in this case: "It is not unusual for them to refuse giving their Apache names when interrogated; but will endeavor to give some Mexican appellative in its place."[31] Corle also has Agocho use the Apache names for the months (December is Sos-nahl-tus, which means "snow coming down"). Occasionally, too, he has Agocho throw out an Apache phrase (Agocho angrily tries to scare white ranchers off land near his spring by saying, "White men go away. Tluh-go nde hi e-na."[32]).

Agocho and Kai-a eat and drink traditionally. For example, Kai-a prepares a meal in which she serves "mesquite beans and fruit from prickly pear cactus."[33] Bourke speaks of "bread made from mesquite beans" and of "the fruit of the giant cactus" as being common Apache foods.[34] Corle tells us that one of the reasons Agocho is attracted to the Salton Sea is that it contains no fish: "An Apache will never eat fish or bear, both foods being a taboo that is never violated."[35] Corle probably learned of this taboo from Reagan,[36] although he could have learned it elsewhere. Similarly, in the preparation of *tizwin,* an intoxicating fermented drink, Agocho uses grain (corn) and techniques (crushing the corn into a pulp, letting it ferment, then adding water) which Corle probably learned about from Reagan.[37]

In matters pertaining to food, however, Corle was no

slave to his sources. Reagan says that the Apache woman has "a pot, skillet or frying pan, a five gallon coal oil can."[38] Kai-a does not acquire these until Agocho brings them home from Petterman's store and contemptuously gives them to her. Before that, because Corle wanted his Apaches to be primitive, Kai-a cooks coyote meat on a stick over a fire. And whereas Reagan says that *tizwin* is used during wild communal drinking parties among the White Mountain Apaches,[39] Corle has Agocho use it instead as part of his son's adolescence ceremony. The extended drinking spree he and his son engage in at the end of the ceremony is designed by Agocho to mark his son's symbolic return to an Apache sense of communalism. In effect, however, it serves ironically as a means for getting this wildly drunken Apache youth out on the highway where he first encounters Maria, the "white" woman who is to be the agent for his final removal from the Apache ways of his father. Corle departs from his sources when his narrative profits from it.

It is interesting to compare Corle's description of building an Apache hut with his source. Reagan says: "The Apache, for the most part, live in circular dome-shaped houses. . . . The Apache house is made entirely by the women. The poles are cut and collected and the covering wholly obtained by them. They are made of a framework of poles and limbs tied together, over which a thatch of brush, yucca leaves, rushes or flags is placed. Over this a canvass is stretched. The structure is open at the top to allow the escape of smoke."[40] Corle makes some slight changes: "Together they constructed the little shelter in a day, building it in a circle converging toward the top but with an opening at the peak for smoke to go through if they ever wished to have a fire inside."[41] We should notice first that Corle omits mentioning the canvass covering, partly because it would be unnecessary in the desert where it hardly ever rains, and partly because Agocho would not have wanted to use a material made by white men. We also should notice that whereas Corle, to be ethnographically precise, should have had Kai-a make the house by herself, he has Agocho and Kai-a do it together. The explanation for this is probably that Kai-a is pregnant, and also that Agocho's other wives are not along on this trip. (Corle, incidentally, is quite right to suggest that Apache men might have had more than one wife.)

Under the circumstances, then, Agocho's sharing of the duties normally reserved for women is entirely acceptable, and it does not mean that Agocho is uncharacteristic of Apaches in his attitude toward women, or that Kai-a is uncharacteristically demanding. Reagan points out that "to the Apache woman falls the greater part of the work. In a very true sense, she is 'bought and paid for' by her husband and he treats her accordingly. She does his every bidding."[42] Agocho does expect Kai-a to do most of the work, and when she questions his account of the formation of the Salton Sea, Agocho "became irritated and told her to shut up."[43] Kai-a is hardworking and passive. She follows her roaming husband without ever seriously questioning his motives or his destination. When they come into Yuma, it is she who unpacks the horses, sets up camp, and prepares the meal, while Agocho chats with his friends. The next morning it is she who gets up before dawn, starts a fire, and begins breakfast. Kai-a is similar to "typical" Apache women also in that she wears a special girdle when she is pregnant, to facilitate labor,[44] and is proficient in the making of baskets.[45] Corle was careful to be accurate, then, in presenting ethnographic details of Apache domestic life. These details are not all presented for their own sake, however. Corle used Kai-a's basket-making as an important element in his plot, for example, for it is when Agocho is in Mecca to trade some extra baskets for cartridges for his rifle that Kai-a is brutally raped and murdered.

Corle also made use of some authentic details of the Apache courtship traditions. Bourke reports that "when an Apache young man begins to feel the first promptings of love for any particular young damsel, he makes known the depth and sincerity of his affection by presenting the young woman with a calico skirt, cut and sewed by his own fair fingers."[46] For Maria Johnny Mack makes, not a skirt, but a necklace of animal teeth. This gift is quite understandably more primitive than a calico skirt, but the idea and the effect are the same.

One of the most dramatic scenes in the novel takes place when Maria passes through the date grove where Johnny Mack is working. Johnny waits for her to return by the same path so that he can give her the necklace. She accepts the necklace and indicates by a touch that she accepts Johnny Mack as well. There ensues an exciting pursuit in which he chases her through the grove. In the end he catches her, and she willingly surrenders herself to him. Surely this is an adaptation of what Corle had read in Reagan's book about how an Apache youth conducts a courtship: "He then becomes the aggressor. He watches her most frequented trail, usually the one over which she carries water. For the furtherance of his object, he places a row of stones in some secluded spot on both sides of this trail. . . . If she passes to the side of the rows of stones it is a refusal; but should she pass on the trail between the stones, it is an acceptance. He then sometimes rushes out, seizes her, and takes her to his camp."[47] Corle changed the details, but kept the essence: Johnny Mack waits near the path along which Maria will soon pass, receives her signal of acceptance, and then seizes her. In many ways Johnny Mack's relationship with Maria, especially as it develops later, is distinctly un-Apache, but at this point in the story Johnny Mack has not yet become fully white in his ways, and it is appropriate that Corle should have him demonstrate at least faint vestiges of his Apache upbringing.

There are other ethnographically accurate details which could be mentioned here, but enough have been mentioned to show that Corle did use authentic material in his novel and that this material provides a core of authenticity for his work. Even though the average reader would have no way of knowing whether all of the details of Apache life were accurate, the very fact that Corle incorporated so many of them lends an air of reality to his novel and appears to anchor the fiction to a solid basis of fact. The appearance of factuality is at least as important to the novelist as the factuality itself, and Corle has done remarkably well on both counts. Not only did Corle not invent most of his ethnographic background material, but he also does not *appear* to have done so.

A CULTURAL BENCHMARK

Corle's use of ethnographic detail does more than lend an air of authenticity and plausibility to *Fig Tree John*. A second important use of such material is to provide a fixed set of cultural traditions and values against which to measure the cultural development of Corle's characters, Agocho and Johnny Mack. If the primary theme of the novel is that the American Indian must give up his old ways and assimilate the new ways, then it is vital that Corle clearly describe those old ways. Having done that, he can then proceed to show that while Agocho continues to follow those old ways, Johnny Mack gives them up and follows new ones.

For example, Agocho builds a round Apache hut out of rough materials and is still living in it at the end of the novel, while Johnny Mack has built a white man's house on the same plot of ground, a rectangular house made out of boards. It is important to note that in 1906 Agocho moves into his new life on a horse, because at the end of the novel, he is still using horses, while Johnny Mack moves into his new life in 1928 in a Ford roadster. It is important to know that the traditional Apache male is fully dominant over his submissive wife, because at the end of the novel, Johnny Mack departs from this tradition and marries a woman who demonstrates more spirit and more independence than Agocho had permitted in Kai-a. It is important to know that Ste-na-tlih-a is the most powerful goddess of the Apaches, because at the end Johnny Mack has forsaken her for the Virgin Mary, her counterpart in the white man's religion. Knowing that Apaches usually lived off the land by hunting and gathering is important, because Johnny lives by working for money on a white man's ranch. Corle needed to show the old Apache ways so that his readers would see that Agocho scarcely departs at all, while Johnny Mack abandons them almost completely.

The ceremonies relating to birth, adolescence, and death are an important aspect of the old Apache ways. Rather than presenting these ceremonies for their own sake merely to show what Apaches were like and how certain ceremonies were performed at important points in their lives, Corle used them to reinforce his theme and his characterization. He used ethnographic background relating to Apache birth, adolescence, and death ceremonies to provide an ironic reversal of the purposes for which the ceremonies were designed, and to provide a symbolic undergirding to Johnny Mack's gradual rejection of the ways those ceremonies represent. Instead of immersing Johnny Mack in Apache ways, the ceremonies actually serve to suggest the stages by which he moves away from them and toward white ways.

It is likely that Corle had read Reagan's account of the typical Apache birth ceremony: "The baby is brought into the world without much ado. . . . An Indian cradle is made for it, usually by the mother. . . . The child is placed in it . . . amid much sprinkling of pollen and praying to the gods for the baby's welfare."[48] What is especially interesting here is that Agocho performs some of the details of the birth ceremony before, not after, his son is born, and that he uses them not for the welfare of the child, but for the welfare of Kai-a, who is still in labor: "He was not exactly sure of what ritual and what ceremony he could evoke to help her. . . . Agocho was limited in this knowledge but he did the best he could with what seemed fitting to the occasion. He scattered pollen to the four winds and then at sunrise he went down to the beach of the Salton Sea. With the Water God at his feet and the Fire God in the sky he said a long prayer to Stena-tlih-a, the mother of both those Gods, so that she would understand and help and protect her earth daughter, Kai-a."[49] When the child is actually born, Agocho performs no birth ceremony at all. In Apache custom, to be sure, this is the job of the midwife and the mother, but instead of filling in for the midwife, Agocho apparently neglects the ceremony altogether. If Corle deliberately has Agocho, in his ignorance, neglect an important Apache ceremony for his son, perhaps he is suggesting that Johnny Mack is destined from the very beginning to grow up to be something quite different from an Apache. Agocho, through his neglect, is helping to bring about what he so much fears.

Agocho's ignorance of traditional Apache ceremonialism is also shown in the adolescence, or puberty, ceremony he devises for his son years later: "Agocho did not have the supreme powers of a medicine man and he knew that at best his efforts would be crude and superficial. At any rate, they would be better than no efforts at all."[50] The adolescence ceremony does not have the effect on Johnny Mack that Agocho hopes it will have, and Corle may be suggesting, again, that part of the fault lies with the fact that the ceremony itself is imperfectly performed. From another point of view, it also is convenient for Corle to have Agocho know so little about the intricate details of Apache ceremonialism: if Agocho does not know the details, then Corle does not need to bog his novel down with them. Still, Corle's account of the Apache adolescence ceremony is remarkably close to his ethnographic sources.

Originally, the male adolescence ceremony was chiefly military in nature. Goddard discusses the ceremony recorded in the White Mountain Apache creation myth: "When a youth went through an adolescence ceremony he did it with a definite career in mind. The normal myth of this type put the emphasis on the weapons secured and feats of warlike prowess in killing the monsters; that is, the warrior idea is uppermost."[51] Goddard is discussing the ceremony as it appears in mythology, but in actuality the male adolescence ceremony was traditionally a military affair, designed primarily to prepare the youth for participation in his first raid.[52] By the 1900s the military function had largely been lost from the adolescence ceremony because of the enforced curtailing of raids and warfare among reservation Apaches. That the ceremony Agocho devises is not military in its pur-

pose, then, is quite understandable. For Agocho the ceremony is designed to instruct his son in the ways of the
Apaches and to counteract the corrupting influence of the
white man. The immediate motivation for it comes from
Johnny Mack's return home one day with the knowledge
that George Washington was the father of his country. This
angers Agocho, for of course he knows that George Washington was not the father of the Apache nation. Agocho
determines to do something to correct his son's ignorance:
"He knew that the boy was ignorant of life, ignorant of
ideals, experience, and ceremonies of tribal living. To some
degree he could correct that and he proposed to do so."[53]

The instructional purpose of the adolescence ceremony
was a legitimate one, as we see in the following brief account
Reagan gives of it: "The boys, when entering the period
of manhood, go off singly or in groups and fast and pray
and perform certain ceremonies prescribed by the medicine-
men to make them strong, courageous men, to secure them
a suitable wife and healthy offspring, and to receive instruction so they can choose their life occupation and their
guardian spirit. The latter appears to them in a dream after
exhaustive fasting and praying and may be any animate or
inanimate thing or something purely imaginary. . . . The
ceremony is closed with an elaborate feast, usually followed
by a prolonged dance."[54] Corle was accurate enough, then,
when he has Agocho devise a ceremony for the purpose of
helping his son "to receive instruction." From Reagan's brief
account Corle also derived suggestions for several other elements of Agocho's ceremony. Agocho sends Johnny Mack
off on the third day to, in Reagan's words, "pray and perform certain ceremonies" after having undergone what Reagan calls "exhaustive fasting." What Reagan describes as
an "elaborate feast" at the end, Agocho makes instead
merely a prolonged *tizwin*-drinking affair. But *tizwin* was
drunk at adolescence ceremonies,[55] and in this case it does
lead naturally into the "prolonged dance" described by
Reagan.

Corle makes two significant additions to the accepted

practice as revealed by Reagan. One is what Agocho calls "the race between the young men and the virgins."[56] This race was, in Agocho's mind, supposed to mark the culmination of the adolescence ceremony. Corle probably got the idea for this race from Reagan's description of the female adolescence ceremony: "When the girl arrives at the threshold of womanhood, she goes through more elaborate ceremonies than the boy, though often not of so private a nature. The females of the vicinity (and sometimes the males) chase her around, heat her up, and then examine her. . . . At Indian Cooley's camp on Cibicu, April fifteenth, 1901, one of the girls was entering womanhood. Just after breakfast the young people chased her all around the premises."[57] No doubt Corle simply transferred this chase to the male ceremony.

The other addition that Corle made is the role of Pollen Boy. Agocho makes a drum for the ceremony and "he put the sign of his clan on one side and a figure representing Hadintin Skhin, Pollen Boy, on the other. Pollen Boy represented youth scattering his seed over the land and was an important figure in a puberty dance."[58] Here again, however, Corle does not depart far from the material at his disposal. He would have learned from Bourke both that pollen was used in virtually every important Apache ceremony and that the term "Hoddentin eshkin," meaning pollen child, appeared in at least one Apache prayer.[59] In bringing together materials from a number of different sources and in adapting them to his own use, Corle made certain changes and altered certain emphases, but he almost always tried to make sure that the information he presented was in keeping with the Apache way of life as he understood it from the sources of information available to him. If what we have in the novel is not always true to the letter of the Apache custom, it is usually true to the spirit of it.

The two chief additions which Corle introduced into the male adolescence ceremony as described by Reagan were probably introduced primarily for literary reasons. The Pollen Boy figure on the drum, represented as a youth scattering his seed over the land, is an ironic reflection of Johnny

Mack himself. Not only does Johnny Mack find employment as a quite different kind of pollen boy when he works for Mr. Mack artificially pollenating the date trees, but, in giving up the Apache way of life and moving away from his father's spring to join his pregnant wife in Banning, he is "scattering his seed over the land." Similarly, the chase of the virgin cannot take place in the way Agocho had intended, but it does take place a little later, in a way Agocho had not intended, when Johnny Mack chases Maria through the date grove. In introducing these two elements into the adolescence ceremony, Corle wanted to show that Agocho's supreme efforts to bring his son back into the Apache fold are doomed to failure, because the world in which the ceremony takes place is not the world Agocho wishes it to be. Pollen Boy still exists, but he takes a non-Apache form. The virgin chase is still a valid, though slightly delayed, part of the ceremony, but the virgin is a "white" girl, not an Apache one.

Corle's most subtle use of this kind of ironic adaptation of the old ceremony to the new world can be found in Johnny Mack's "vision." According to Reagan, one purpose of the male ceremony was to provide a means for the Apache youth to see and accept his "guardian spirit," his "guiding spirit." This spirit would appear to him "in a dream after exhaustive fasting and praying."[60] Johnny Mack does receive his "guiding spirit" during the ceremony, for after drinking a little too much *tizwin* he wanders out to the highway at night and there receives a "vision" of Maria, the girl he is later to marry. Once again Agocho's ceremony works in ways he has not anticipated, ways which serve to undermine the very purpose for which Agocho had intended it. Maria, of course, "guides" Johnny Mack further away from Apache customs, and, because of Johnny's confused association of Maria with the Virgin Mary of the white man's religion, she also leads him away from the Apache religion.

Corle uses the traditional Apache adolescence ceremony, then, not as it was intended to be used by Agocho, but ironically. Johnny does achieve manhood and independence through the ceremony, but the effect is ultimately the direct opposite of Agocho's intended purpose. By taking part in the ceremony designed to mark the end of his adolescence and to mark his return to tribal ways, Johnny Mack ends his adolescence by rejecting still further those tribal ways.

Early in his life Johnny Mack learns about the Apache death ceremony, for his mother dies when he is quite young. His father insists, however, that he participate in the ritual. The ritual which Agocho devises is largely, as near as we can tell, Corle's own invention. Corle undoubtedly got from Reagan the idea for having Agocho "wrap the deceased in a blanket"[61] before burying the body. From Bourke he probably picked up the notion that Apaches "believe that the dead remain for a few days or nights in the neighborhood of the place where they departed from this life,"[62] and this probably led him to have Agocho not cover the grave with stones until four days after the interrment so that the spirit could escape from the grave. From Cremony he probably learned that Apaches sometimes try to put off dealing with a death "from a desire to escape the duty of performing the dreaded burial service,"[63] for Corle has Agocho stall until "there was no other duty he could attend to first — no other excuse for waiting — no reason, now for not attending to the ruined kowa, and to her."[64] Many of the burial procedures in the novel, however, would not have been characteristic of traditional Apache ways.

Most of Agocho's deviations from standard Apache burial practice are fully explained by the special circumstances of Kai-a's death. The White Mountain Apaches would generally bury their dead in "some crevice in the rocks,"[65] whereas Agocho, miles from those Arizona crevices, digs a grave in the desert sands. Apaches would normally "burn the house of the deceased and everything in it,"[66] but in this case the house has already been burned to the ground. Agocho's explanation to his son that his mother's spirit "would travel on the Milky Way to heaven"[67] is not official Apache doctrine. Indeed, there does not appear to have been one accepted explanation of such things among

Apaches. In this case, however, it may be merely a little story Agocho makes up to try to explain to his young son the mystery of death. Deviations like this, then, need not detain us.

The only apparently significant changes which Corle makes from traditional Apache burial practice are, first, that Agocho takes so seriously his dead wife's burial and, second, that he keeps a four-day vigil at the gravesite. Cremony tells this story: "One day an Apache woman died in camp, and I asked Gian-nah-tah if there would be much lamentation. He simply smiled at the idea, and replied: 'It was a woman; her death is of no account.' "[68] There is no suggestion that Agocho considers the death of his wife to be a matter of "no account," and he takes her burial ceremony most seriously. There are two explanations for this. For one thing, Kai-a is not, under these circumstances, just "an Apache woman"; she is Agocho's only grown companion, so he would naturally feel her loss with more than usual poignancy. For another thing, his sincere grieving at her death is important literarily in that many of Agocho's significant actions in the remainder of the novel are governed by his desire to avenge her death. His monomaniacal drive for vengeance would not be convincing if Agocho had in any sense belittled the importance of Kai-a's death.

Similarly, the four-day graveside vigil would have been unheard of for Apaches. Apaches would have been most anxious to get far away from the grave as soon as possible. I believe that the explanation for Corle's invention is that he wanted to provide a ceremony that was simple yet substantial enough so that Johnny Mack would remember it and be able to repeat it for his father two decades later. The digging of the grave, the placing of stones on the mound, the four days of waiting beside the grave all provide an entirely fitting end to Agocho's earthly existence. The last of the old Apaches receives what, in terms of this novel at least, is an old Apache death ceremony.

Just as the other ceremonies give symbolic support to Johnny Mack's movement away from the Apache ways of his father, so does this final death ceremony. The absence of a birth ceremony for Johnny Mack suggests that he never received the proper introduction to Apache life. His adolescence ceremony really marks his growth to independence from his Apache background, rather than his immersion in that background. And now, at the end, the death ceremony he performs for his father marks the final death of any remnants of Apache tradition and loyalty left in him. The death of Agocho is symbolically the death of the Apache in Johnny Mack: "Johnny wasn't Apache, but Agocho had been, and that ceremony *had* to be right. . . . Johnny was white now."[69] Corle, then, makes careful use of Apache ceremonialism to suggest human development, especially Johnny Mack's human development away from the culture which that ceremonialism represents.

A QUESTION OF MOTIVATION

Corle's third, and most important, way of using the ethnographic sources at his disposal was to provide an explanation for some of Agocho's otherwise inexplicable attitudes and unmotivated actions. Writing primarily for a white audience which had little or no firsthand experience with the American Indian, Corle relied upon his readers' willing suspension of disbelief in matters pertaining to the "Apache mind." Rather than providing a strictly logical explanation for all of Agocho's actions and attitudes, Corle implied that such actions and attitudes were just typically Apache. This method was not entirely satisfactory, of course. We have already seen that Corle never makes it quite clear why Agocho would migrate to the Salton Sea from central Arizona, or why he would hate white men so unreservedly even *before* they rape and murder his wife. And in suggesting that the "Apache mind" is somehow basically different from other minds, or that Apache nature is somehow different from human nature, Corle shows what seems in the 1970s to be a curiously antiquated conception of what Indians are like. We should bear in mind, however, that Corle was writing in the early 1930s, and that both he and his audience were of an age when "unenlightened" attitudes about Indians were both acceptable and prevalent. Indeed, Corle found support for some of these attitudes in his ethnographic sources, and it is clear that he relied on the then-current theoretical and experiential thinking about Apaches as a foundation for certain elements in Agocho's character.

Right from the beginning Corle asserts Agocho's dislike for white men. In the second paragraph of the first chapter, when Agocho is coming into Yuma, we are told that Agocho displays "no interest in the white civilization."[70] He very much enjoys the story of how the "River Spirit" plays a trick on "these stupid white men" who try to turn the river into the desert.[71] That night Agocho dreams "of huge avalanches of water sweeping the white men and all their property in a turmoil before them while a great crowd of Apaches watched and drank and laughed. It was a very happy time."[72] Instead of explaining the reasons for Agocho's dislike of white men and his pleasure at their discomfort, Corle seems to suggest that it was just an Apache trait to feel this way. He could easily have picked up support for this notion from Cremony: "From earliest infancy they are instructed to regard every other race as natural enemies. Their suspicions and savage distrust are aroused and cultivated before they ever come in contact with other people. An Apache child of three years will run and yell with fear and hate from a white man. Apache mothers hush their children by naming an American."[73] If we accept such a view of the Apache character, as Corle apparently did for the purposes of this novel, then we will not question the specific motivation for such statements in the novel as these: "he didn't like white men";[74] "they were all a race of blundering fools";[75] "they were never trustworthy."[76]

Similarly, the idea for Agocho's arrogant refusal to consider adopting any of the ways of the white man may have originated in Corle's reading of his ethnographic sources. Cremony speaks of the Apache's "inveterate opposition to all innovation."[77] Reagan speaks of the efforts of the Apaches to keep their children out of the white man's schools: "About two weeks before school each fall they inaugurated medicine dances and kept the children in constant turmoil to wear them out — they said it was done to make the child medicine-proof against the white man's ways and medicines. Sometimes they would dip them in the cold water of the creeks and hold them there to make sure that they would be too sick to be admitted to school."[78] Corle has Agocho refuse to let Mrs. Reeves enroll his son in the white man's school and resist all outside influences on his way of life. At least for the purposes of this novel, Corle apparently considered it to be quite "Apache" to feel this way.

An important aspect of Agocho's character, and one which controls much of the action after the rape and murder of Kai-a, is his burning need for vengeance combined with his patient waiting for the chance to achieve it. The insistence upon vengeance was so well-known as an Apache trait that Corle need not have relied on his sources for verification. All he had to do was find ways to remind his readers of the Apache demand for revenge in order to render plausible Agocho's driving desire for it. He does this by emphasizing Agocho's delight early in the novel that the River Spirit had gotten revenge on the white men who had tried to turn it out of its natural course: "the foolish white men . . . had received their just punishment for interfering with a Great Spirit."[79] Similarly, later in the novel, Agocho recalls the time Qulba Bachu had murdered Agocho's uncle for stealing his wife. This revenge was entirely appropriate among the Apaches. Indeed, the other Apaches had thought Qulba Bachu was a coward until the day that he shot Agocho's uncle ten times. Agocho's willingness to wait patiently for nearly two decades to avenge his wife's death was more difficult to explain than his mere desire for revenge, but Corle was careful to provide at least one precedent for it in the case of Qulba Bachu. Qulba Bachu had waited four years before murdering Agocho's uncle, even though he could have done so at any time prior to that. Qulba Bachu was in no hurry and simply waited until he was ready. He knew all the while that "he had the right to shoot him."[80] Like Qulba Bachu before him, Agocho is willing to bide his time, for in his supreme pride he knows that the gods will provide him with the opportunity.

This supreme pride is one of Agocho's most important characteristics. Agocho, Corle tells us, "lived by his own code and that code made him the center of the universe."[81] In Agocho, "the ego was everything. . . . This megalomania reached a climax of self-exaltation. The world was his. He was absolute. . . . Perhaps he was a God."[82] Agocho interprets everything in terms of himself. All experience is to be explained in terms of its usefulness or its relevance to his own needs and existence, and he rationalizes whatever happens to him or around him to make it fit into a divine plan which is working itself out for his benefit. I suspect that Corle got the basic idea for this aspect of Agocho's character from Cremony: "The teachings of experience are lost upon the Apache. He believes himself the superior being, and frequent adversities are accounted for in so many and plausible ways that his self-love and inordinate vanity are always appeased."[83] Corle may not have accepted so broad a generalization about the characteristic pride of the Apache, but it is clear that he used Cremony's statement as a starting point for his development of Agocho's arrogant and self-centered pride.

That pride finds concrete expression in Agocho's interpretation of "signs" from the gods. In treating Agocho's trust in and interpretation of these signs, Corle made what is probably his greatest departure from the known facts of Apache custom. In this case it is not so much that Corle purposefully changed what was known, as that he invented elements in the Apache religious system to fill in where the record was incomplete.

In fact, very little was known about Apache religion when Corle was writing, or about the relationship between an individual Apache and his "gods." Perhaps Corle had read Bourke's statement that "the taciturnity of the Apache in regard to all that concerns their religious ideas is a very marked feature of their character; probably no tribe with which our people have come in contact has succeeded more thoroughly in preserving from profane inquiry a complete knowledge of matters relating to their beliefs and ceremonials."[84] Bourke also expresses his concern that so little effort had been made to understand the mental workings of the Apache: "Nothing has been so neglected by the Americans as an examination into the mental processes by which an Indian arrives at his conclusions, the omens, auguries, hopes and fears by which he is controlled and led to one extreme or the other in all that he does."[85] If Corle had read these passages, he would have learned that if he wanted to say much about the "religious ideas" or the "mental processes" of Apaches he would have to invent it. So he did.

Agocho is sensitive to signs from the supreme powers, and he seeks to interpret what would appear to most of us to be natural or accidental phenomena as if they are messages designed to direct his actions. When Agocho sets up his camp at the spring near the Salton Sea, things go so well that he thinks "the Great Spirits were kind" to him and Kai-a and "must have been pleased with them."[86] Then he goes down to the beach and listens "to the voices of the Gods in the song of the wind and the lap of the water"; these voices tell him "that his wife would bear him a son in this place, and that the fig trees would grow, and that the Gods of fire and water would watch over him and protect him as long as he remained."[87] These "voices" are what convince Agocho that he should stay, for if he does stay he can be sure that the supreme powers will watch over him and direct his actions. Agocho's interpretation is a very subjective one, but it is nonetheless real to him.

Later in the novel, Corle describes Agocho as being "caught up in the circular philosophy of cause and effect as determined by a supreme fatalism."[88] But it is not circular from Agocho's point of view, and the fatalism is not negative or fearsome. Agocho's fatalism is a very positive and hopeful conviction that the "gods" will consistently and carefully look after him and direct his actions. Although Agocho is sometimes puzzled and frustrated by their slowness to act on his behalf, and although he is sometimes annoyed by his own apparent inability to interpret their signs correctly, he never ceases for long to trust that the gods will direct him to eventual triumph over his enemies.

While Corle does use these subjectively interpreted signs from the gods to help motivate Agocho's decision to stay at the Salton Sea, the signs serve mainly to motivate Agocho's actions with respect to his enemies. Agocho's faith in the gods gives him the patience to wait for his much-desired revenge. While chasing the white men who are responsible for his wife's death, he finds a knife that they have abandoned and sees it as a "good omen" for "the Gods meant that he should use that knife."[89] When the white men escape on the train, he blames not the gods but his own inability to interpret them: "the Gods meant something else."[90] Even six years later he has not yet figured out what the gods intend for him to do. He tries to "pick up some message from the Gods" but finally concludes merely that "they wanted him to wait."[91] At one point he is about to leave the spring and go back to Arizona, but then, when he is all packed, a deluge strikes his camp, the first rainfall in the desert in five years. To Agocho this is a sign from the gods that "he was about to do the wrong thing," and so he unpacks his horses and resolves never again to "make the slightest effort to move back to his own White River country."[92]

One of the most important signs in the novel involves the stone altar Agocho builds near the palm trees he finds in the hills. He has never seen such trees before, and so he knows that they are "some message from the Gods, naturally."[93] What the message is, however, he cannot discover. He decides to build a stone altar there as a "gesture of homage": "Agocho built a mound of stones about as high as his knees. On the top of it he put a few twigs in the sign of his clan."[94] Corle learned about such Apache altars from Reagan: "The altars in various parts of the Reservation usually consist of a pile of stone on which twigs and shingle rock are placed."[95] The altar, then, is genuine, but Corle adapts it to his own use. According to Reagan, such altars are designed for use as places at which to offer thanks for such things as a task completed or a much-needed rainfall. For Agocho, however, the altar becomes a vehicle for a divine message to himself. Years later Agocho returns to the place where he had built the altar and finds the altar torn down and the rocks scattered. He is convinced that the altar had been "scattered by the Gods. That was a sign. That meant something. That was a message. . . . The Gods have given a command."[96] Agocho interprets the message quite sub-jectively. The command is that he is finally to get his revenge by going home and raping Maria.

With that sign from the gods, the whole divine plan becomes clear to Agocho: "They had driven his son white. He couldn't understand why, but now it was obvious. They had sent his son out into white civilization in spite of Agocho, and they had made his son an instrument in the progress of the scheme. Without either of them knowing it N'Chai Chidn had been an agent of justice all the time."[97] Johnny Mack's "going white," then, had all been a part of the plan of the gods to provide Maria as a proper object for Agocho's revenge, and as someone to take care of his physical and sexual needs.[98] Maria was a gift of the gods "to work for them and cook for them and sleep with them. . . . The ways of the Gods were always plain to see if you had the perspi-cacity to look."[99]

Agocho's reliance on "signs" from the gods may not be an ethnographically accurate Apache trait, but it serves Corle's purposes in this novel. Not only does it provide moti-vation for several of Agocho's most important actions, but it also serves to reinforce Corle's theme by establishing, unambiguously, the cause of Agocho's failure to adjust to the new world: his pride. We readers may not be convinced that the gods really do speak to men in the fashion that Agocho thinks they do, but Corle never expected us to be convinced of that. The point is that Agocho is so arrogantly sure that his way — and his way alone — has the stamp of divine approval that he, like Captain Ahab before him, must be dealt a death-blow by the very forces he is trying in his presumptuously prideful way to destroy. Ahab had sought vengeance by attacking a white whale which turned out to be bigger and more indestructible than he was; Agocho seeks vengeance by attacking a white society which turns out to be bigger and more indestructible than he is. Both men fail, but both men are magnificent in their failure.

LITERARY EVALUATION

It is clear, then, that Corle relied heavily on biographical and ethnographic facts in composing his novel, but it is even more clear that he was no slave to the factual material he took the trouble to uncover. We must now consider the implications for literary criticism of the comparisons I have been making between fact and fiction, for Corle has been both praised for writing an accurate book and criticized for writing an inaccurate one.

As for the latter point, there is no question that Corle's portrait of Fig Tree John is far from being biographically reliable, and we can appreciate the annoyance of Juanito Razon's friends, acquaintances, and relatives that Corle used the name of Fig Tree John and a skeleton of biographical facts about him as the basis for what Shumway called a "libelous fabrication." We may wonder, indeed, why Corle did not change the names of his white and Indian characters, if only to avoid possible lawsuits. Johnny Mack, especially, might have had grounds for claiming defamation of character on the basis of Corle's having had him murder his father with an ax. That murder never happened in real life, and Corle surely knew it. Nevertheless, while biographical inaccuracy may be sound basis for the annoyance of some readers, it is clearly no basis for saying that the novel is in itself faulty. Similarly, the ethnographic "mistakes" Corle makes may be cause for the amusement of knowing anthropologists, or the annoyance of Apaches, but these mistakes, most of them conscious ones on Corle's part, are no reason to call *Fig Tree John* a bad novel. Any novel has its own right to independent existence, quite apart from the verifiability of the "facts" which it posits.

Just as it is unfair to criticize Corle's novel because it contains biographical and ethnographic inaccuracies, so it is unfair to criticize it for the outdated theme it conveys. Corle must appear to many readers in the 1970s to be something of a racist. His theme — that Indians must be flexible, that they must make some accommodation to the dominant white culture which has overshadowed their native culture — is no longer acceptable to most readers knowledgeable about Indian affairs. The current feeling is that the Indian cultures are worth preserving, and that Indians should do all they can to resist white ways. The Johnny Macks of today, the Indians who are ready and willing to adopt the white man's ways and to reject tribal ones, are contemptuously referred to as "Uncle Tomahawks" or as "Apples" (red on the outside, white on the inside).

Corle could be defended against charges that he is a racist or a white supremacist. It could be pointed out, for example, that Corle does not suggest in the novel that the whites are *better* than the Indians, only that their presence is a political and cultural reality which Indians, realistically, cannot ignore. Or it could be pointed out that when Corle wrote the novel, in the days before John Collier's views had gained much sway,[100] Corle would have been considered rather liberal. In a time when the true racists were still arguing for extermination or enforced incarceration of Indians, Corle was arguing that, if Indians were sufficiently flexible, they could — and should — become assimilated into the American melting pot.

Corle's novel, however, can be defended on more general grounds, for the political acceptability of an author's point of view is essentially irrelevant to an evaluation of his creative products.

If it is true that we must not find fault with *Fig Tree John* for the wrong reasons, so, too, we should be careful not to praise it for the wrong reasons. The novel has been widely praised, but much of the praise has been of questionable validity. Pilkington has been most enthusiastic about the book. He says that *Fig Tree John* shows that Corle was "a remarkable human being, a man who saw, truly and clearly, the configuration of the Indian's world and had no desire either to romanticize it or re-arrange it."[101] There is little doubt that Corle was remarkable, and it does not appear that he romanticized his portrait of Fig Tree John, if by that we mean that he sentimentalized it. It is clear, however, that Corle did drastically "re-arrange" the real Fig Tree John and his world. Similarly, when critics praise Corle for his acute "analysis of Agocho's mind,"[102] for being one who "knows his Indians from the inside,"[103] and for being able to take his readers "into the psychology . . . of the Indian,"[104] we must not forget that Agocho's mind is not necessarily a "real" Indian mind; certainly it is not Juanito Razon's. This kind of praise, therefore, is both inaccurate and misleading.

Corle has also been praised for remaining neutral in *Fig Tree John*. The portrait of Agocho, we are told, is "objective."[105] Corle "makes no judgments at all,"[106] and "does not appear to take sides."[107] One of the things which a comparison of the lives of Juanito Razon and Agocho, the "real" and the "created" Fig Tree Johns, makes clear is that, on the contrary, Corle is not neutral. He emphatically does take sides and does present his own strongly felt views in this novel. Far from being objective, Corle's portrait of Fig Tree John is carefully drawn to show the terrible consequences of a man's refusal to adjust to the realities of life. Corle wanted to demonstrate the misery, the misunderstanding, and even the physical danger involved when a man refuses to change his habitual way of doing things and seeing the world around him. He wanted to show, specifically, that for an Apache to deny the encroachments and the culture of the white man must mean the death of the Apache by violent means. Corle wanted to show in fiction what he was later to explain in essay form about Apache character: "The Apache . . . was an extremist in everything. . . . Fanaticism and obsession made the Apache fight with insane fury. It was all or nothing; it was win or die."[108] Agocho could not win, so he must die — not in bed from influenza as his real-life counterpart had, but at the hands of one who had come to represent the white point of view. Corle wanted to show in fiction what he was still later to report in essay form about the solution for Apaches in the twentieth century: "There is an answer to the Apache problem, and it is the only answer to any racial minority within the United States — assimilation."[109] Johnny Mack is the Apache who finds this answer in the novel. He trades the goddess Ste-na-tlih-a for the Virgin Mary, the isolated camp for the city, the hunt for the job, the horse for the car. He has assimilated the white man's culture: "Johnny wasn't Apache. . . . Johnny was white now."[110] The dinosaur dies out, and the mutant which has developed the necessary flexibility lives on. I believe that Corle shows sympathy, understanding, and even love for Agocho, but he was neither neutral nor objective in telling us of his life.

Similarly, to call *Fig Tree John* "one of the best studies of the white man's weaknesses as perceived by the red man"[111] is at the very most only part of the truth, for *Fig Tree John* is much more emphatically a study of one red man's weaknesses and limitations as perceived by a white man. For Corle to take sides, to want to make a point, to present a theme, of course, is entirely appropriate. Novelists have done so for centuries. It becomes offensive only if it is too overt. Even though few contemporary readers would agree with Corle that assimilation is the only solution to the "Apache problem," few would find the novel to be "thesis-ridden." Corle's point is made, for the most part, subtly and with respect for those who cannot or will not assimilate.

Whereas the historian, the biographer, and the ethnographer are professionally bound to be inductive in dealing with the Indian, the novelist can be deductive. The former must look first and most attentively at the demonstrably accurate facts, and draw conclusions or generalizations directly from them. The novelist, on the other hand, often has a different approach. He may decide what conclusions or generalizations he wants his readers to draw, and then go about emphasizing the facts and creating the characters which will demonstrate his theme. Corle's responsibility in *Fig Tree John* was neither to the known facts of Juanito Razon's life and character nor to the known facts of Apache culture. These, as we have seen, he pretty much disregarded in favor of his own set of "facts." Corle's responsibility was, instead, to suggest a responsible theme through plausible action and characterization.

Our evaluation of Corle's novel should be based on whether it effectively does what it set out to do. In my view, *Fig Tree John* is a remarkably good novel. To be sure, there are flaws in it — mostly the kinds of flaws one would expect from a 28-year-old writer working rapidly on a first novel: not all the actions are fully motivated (why does Agocho migrate? why does Joe set fire to the hut?); ages and dates do not always coincide (is Johnny two or three when his mother is killed?); the narrative point of view is sometimes uncontrolled and heavy-handed (as in the jab at ethnologists); certain characters are stereotyped (Mrs. Reeves, for example); and one occasionally gets the feeling that Agocho himself is more a symbol of "the orthodox Indian" than an individualized human being.

For the most part, however, Corle knew what he wanted to say in the novel, and he said it effectively. He wanted to show what happened when a man refused to accommodate himself to the modern world. Corle was sure of his theme, and he carefully created a character, a setting, a cultural backdrop, and a series of actions which would effectively convey that theme. It seems ironical that, for a novel which set out to demonstrate the disastrous effects of an Indian's refusal to merge into the dominant white society, Corle used as his model an Indian whose real life demonstrated, on the contrary, that an Indian could successfully adjust to a new kind of life in a dominantly white society. The irony is less striking, however, when we recall that Corle did not really ignore the true characteristics of his model, Juanito Razon; rather, he transferred many of them to Fig Tree

John's son, the Johnny Mack of the novel. It is Johnny Mack who demonstrates what Juanito Razon had demonstrated in real life — that an Indian can merge gracefully into contemporary life in a predominantly white America. When Corle transferred these characteristics to the son, then he had to rely on his creative imagination to develop the character of Agocho as a man who would convincingly demonstrate the fate of a cultural holdout — a desert dinosaur.

Edwin Corle's *Fig Tree John* is still worth reading forty years after its publication, not only because it is an excellent novel, but also because, when read in conjunction with the background materials out of which it grew, it shows us how at least one serious novelist went about incorporating factual materials into fiction.

What becomes most emphatically clear from this study is that facts are rarely directly transferable into fiction. Rarely does a "true-life experience" have the necessary ordering, focus, poignancy, or dramatic quality to serve, directly and without alteration, the purposes of the creative novelist. A biography — the kind of writing I have done in Part One — may be interesting, illuminating, and worthwhile. A description of the lifeways of a tribe of Indians — the kind of writing Reagan has done on the White Mountain Apaches — may also be interesting, illuminating, and worthwhile. But, although both biographical and ethnographic studies may be of use to a novelist who wants to write a piece of fiction, he will almost certainly find that he has to omit some of the facts available to him, to alter others, and at times to invent entirely new "facts," both to fill in gaps in the record and to develop themes and characterizations which are important to the artistic integrity of his own work. If he is to make use of the novelist's two freedoms (to portray individual human feelings and to develop responsible themes), and if he is to live up to the novelist's two responsibilities (to make the story plausible and to motivate the actions of the characters), then he will find that he must select, alter, and invent.

A consideration of Fig Tree John's pride provides an emphatic example of the kinds of changes Corle had to make in his fictional account of the last decades in Fig Tree John's life. Juanito Razon had been a proud man. He felt that he was as good as any man. He refused to be victimized by white men, proudly demanding his dollar when they wanted to take his picture, and proudly refusing to move from lands he knew he had a right to live on. Edwin Corle was aware of this healthy and life-sustaining pride in Juanito Razon, but he felt that to develop his theme about the necessity for human adaptability, he needed his own Fig Tree John to be staunchly unadaptable. As a result, he gave to Agocho an unhealthy and destructive pride to help account for his refusal to adapt to life in a changing world. Having made this basic change in the nature of his subject's pride, Corle then felt the novelist's need to explain it, to intensify it, and to raise it to a higher level of significance.

To explain Agocho's pride, Corle made him a self-reliant and aggressive Apache rather than a peaceful and cooperative Cahuilla. He used the traditional Apache hatred of and resistance to the white man as a basis for Agocho's contemptuous distrust of all things white, and for his proud assurance that his own ways were better.

To intensify this pride, Corle introduced into the plot an entirely new element, the brutal rape and murder of Agocho's wife. The introduction of this element brought into play another trait traditionally associated with Apaches, vengefulness. The rest of the novel is essentially the story of Agocho's quest for revenge. The desire for revenge is, of course, an aspect of pride, for Agocho says, in effect, "No man can do this to *me* and get away with it. Other Indians may cower before these terrible white men, but *I* shall not. *I* shall get even."

To raise this pride to a higher degree of significance, Corle gave it cosmic overtones by having Agocho view his actions as being directed by the gods. This is not simply an Indian trying to get even with a white man; this is a man who thinks he is performing the will of the gods, who in his supreme pride even suspects that he *is* a god. This is not that Indian of fact who built a fence around his spring and proudly proclaimed to the world, "This place is mine." Nor is it that Indian of fact who would have learned in the little Catholic church on the reservation that pride is the foremost of the Seven Deadly Sins and would lead to the fire. This is a man who shares with other powerful literary creations, such as Oedipus, Macbeth, and Ahab, what the Greeks called *hubris,* a highly intense pride which brings down even the greatest of men.

Edwin Corle based his novel on biographical facts, and he was remarkably faithful in depicting the facts of Apache culture. He found, however, that he had to sacrifice a measure of factuality to gain a measure of artistry. We all gain because he made that sacrifice.

NOTES TO TEXT

IN FACT

Notes to pages 4–10

1. Frances Anthony, "Below Sea-Level," *The Land of Sunshine,* 15 (July 1901): 24–25.
2. Nina Paul Shumway and Leland Yost, "Fig Tree John's Gun Was Never Loaded," *Desert Magazine,* 4 (January 1941): 6; article reprinted in full in Part Two.
3. Letter from Edwin Corle to Lawrence Clark Powell, February 18, 1953; letter reprinted in full in Part Two.
4. Shumway and Yost, p. 6.
5. Edward H. Davis, *Edward H. Davis and the Indians of the Southwestern United States and Northwest Mexico,* ed. Charles Russell Quinn and Elena Quinn (Downey, California: Elena Quinn, Publisher, 1965), p. 112.
6. J. Smeaton Chase, *California Desert Trails* (Boston: Houghton Mifflin, 1919), p. 214. At about the same time, Juanito Razon told another visitor that he was born on Section 19 (see the January 16, 1917, letter from Special Commissioner Terrell to Commissioner of Indian Affairs, reprinted in Part One). This little lie, however, was probably designed to impress upon the government agent Juanito Razon's right to ownership of the land.
7. See especially William Duncan Strong, *Aboriginal Society in Southern California,* University of California Publications in American Archaeology and Ethnology (Berkeley: University of California Press, 1929), 26: 49.
8. Shumway and Yost, p. 6.
9. Louise T. Werner, "We Climbed Rabbit Peak," *Desert Magazine,* 15 (September 1952): 18.
10. Retta E. Ewers, "Fig Tree John," *Palm Springs Villager,* February 1953, p. 24.
11. See letter, reprinted in Part One, from Superintendent Coggeshall to Commissioner of Indian Affairs, January 13, 1914.
12. Letter from Lowell John Bean to author, January 9, 1974.
13. Letter from Horatio N. Rust to Commissioner of Indian Affairs, May 13, 1892, 52nd. Congress, 1st. Session, Senate Executive Document no. 108 (Washington: Government Printing Office, 1892), p. 5.
14. Chase, p. 182.
15. Anthony, p. 25.

16. Nevada C. Colley, *From Maine to Mecca* (Indio, California, 1967), pp. 156, 225.

17. Jocie Wallace, "On the Desert," *The Youth's Instructor,* October 17, 1905, p. 2.

18. Strong, p. 49.

19. *San Bernardino Sun,* October 9, 1906.

20. Davis, p. 112.

21. Ulysses S. Grant IV, "A Midsummer Motoring Trip," *Historical Society of Southern California Quarterly,* 43 (March 1961): 90.

22. Shumway and Yost, p. 5. Johnny Mack's testimony has been accepted by many later writers: for example, see Werner, p. 18; Ewers, p. 24; and Harry C. James, *The Cahuilla Indians* (Los Angeles: Westernlore Press, 1960), p. 133.

23. Ross McWhirter and Norris McWhirter, eds., *The Guinness Book of World Records* (Enfield, Middlesex: Guinness Superlatives, Ltd., 1971), p. 16.

24. These letters are in the files of the Bureau of Indian Affairs agency at Riverside, California.

25. See the January 16, 1917, letter of Special Commissioner Terrell to the Commissioner of Indian Affairs, reprinted in Part One. It is interesting to note that Terrell thought 97 to be an inflated figure; he estimated an age of between 80 and 90 for Juanito Razon in 1917.

26. William P. Blake, "Geological Report," *Reports of Explorations and Surveys to Ascertain the Most Practicable and Economical Route for a Railroad from the Mississippi River to the Pacific Ocean,* 33rd. Congress, 2nd. Session, House of Representatives Executive Document no. 91 (Washington: A. O. P. Nicholson, Printer, 1856), p. 98.

27. Anthony, p. 25.

28. Grant, p. 94.

29. Wallace, p. 2.

30. Ewers, p. 24; Colley, p. 123.

31. Wallace, p. 2. It is not entirely clear what she means by "the Kansas and Arizona school." I assume that two separate schools are meant, probably the Haskell Institute in Kansas and the Phoenix Indian School in Arizona. All other information in this paragraph comes from the Bureau of Indian Affairs files on Juanito Razon and from Louisa Aguilar.

32. Shumway and Yost, p. 7.

33. Colley, p. 123.

34. June A. W. McCarroll, "Fig Tree John's Uniform," *Desert Magazine,* 4 (October 1941): 2.

35. Letter from Mrs. Otho Moore to author, January 24, 1974.

36. Letter from Jack R. Taylor to author, February 4, 1974. I have not been able to locate the article Mr. Taylor referred to from the *Los Angeles Times.*

37. Letter from Cecelia Foulkes to author, January 20, 1974.

38. Shumway and Yost, p. 7.

39. Letter from Melvin Bisbee to author, January 17, 1974.

40. *Desert Barnacle and Coachella Valley Submarine,* October 29, 1949, p. 10.

41. Ewers, p. 24.

42. Anthony, pp. 24–25.

43. Colley, p. 226.

44. Chase, p. 181.

45. Shumway and Yost, p. 6.

46. Grant, pp. 90, 94–95; see also the newspaper clipping reprinted in Part One in the November 3, 1913, letter from Special Agent Kelsey to Commissioner of Indian Affairs.

47. Shumway and Yost, p. 7.

48. John Hilton, "Paradise for Hammer Hounds," *Desert Magazine,* 5 (January 1942): 18.

49. Edith Carlson, "The Death Bed Map of a Lost Desert Gold Mine," *Palm Springs Villager,* September 1951, p. 15.

50. Philip A. Bailey, *Golden Mirages* (New York: Macmillan, 1940), p. 110.

51. H. E. Marshall as told to W. A. Linkletter, "Peg Leg Gold Secret Hidden with Fig Tree John in Death," *Palm Springs Villager,* March 1955, pp. 17–18.

52. The full letter from Mrs. C. D. Brauckman to Special Agent H. E. Wadsworth, July 8, 1929, is reprinted in Part One.

53. Werner, pp. 18–19. Although she mentions Pegleg Smith, Werner refers to the mine as an Indian mine, not as the famous Pegleg mine. Marshall's account connecting Juanito Razon directly with the Pegleg mine was not published until three years later.

54. Wallace, p. 2.

55. Chase, pp. 182–83.

56. Wallace, p. 2.

57. Harry C. James, "Fig Tree John," *True West,* June 1961, p. 18.

58. James, *Cahuilla Indians,* p. 131.

59. Shumway and Yost, p. 7.

60. Letter from W. F. Beal to D. R. Landis, February 22, 1917; Bureau of Indian Affairs file, Riverside, California.

61. Grant, p. 95.

62. Colley, p. 156.

63. Letter from Superintendent Ellis to O. J. Mitchell, October 23, 1923; reprinted in Part One.

64. From the letter from Superintendent Burris to Commissioner of Indian Affairs, March 23, 1920; reprinted in Part One.

65. Letter from Jack R. Taylor to author, February 4, 1974.

66. Shumway and Yost, p. 7.

67. Letter from Superintendent Coggeshall to Commissioner of Indian Affairs, January 13, 1914; reprinted in Part One.

68. Werner, p. 18.

69. Lowell John Bean and Harry Lawton, *The Cahuilla Indians of Southern California,* Malki Museum Brochure no. 1 (Banning, California: Malki Museum Press, 1965) [pp. 3–4].

70. Report of S. S. Lawson to Commissioner of Indian Affairs, August 20, 1881, *Annual Report of the Commissioner of Indian Affairs to the Secretary of the Interior for the Year 1881* (Washington: Government Printing Office, 1881), p. 14.

71. Letter from Horatio N. Rust to Commissioner of Indian Affairs, February 4, 1891, 52nd. Congress, 1st. Session, Senate Executive Document no. 108 (Washington: Government Printing Office, 1892), p. 14.

72. A copy of the General Allotment Act is handily available in Edward H. Spicer, *A Short History of the Indians of the United States* (New York: D. Van Nostrand, 1969), pp. 200–04.

73. Letter from Cecelia Foulkes to author, January 20, 1974.

74. Letter from Lowell John Bean to author, January 9, 1974.

IN FICTION

Notes to pages 73–86

1. Frederick Manfred in the *Minneapolis Tribune* for May 23, 1971, p. E9.

2. Walter James Miller, "Introduction" to *Fig Tree John* (New York: Liveright, 1971), p. ix.

3. William T. Pilkington, "Edwin Corle and the Southwestern Indian," *Western Review,* 4 (Winter 1967): 52.

4. Nina Paul Shumway, *Your Desert and Mine* (Los Angeles: Westernlore Press, 1960), p. 41.

5. Nina Paul Shumway and Leland Yost, "Fig Tree John's Gun Was Never Loaded," *Desert Magazine* 4 (January 1941): 5–7.

6. The "Dr. Hodge" referred to in the next-to-last paragraph was Frederick Webb Hodge, director of the Southwest Museum in Los Angeles, and one of America's most distinguished and knowledgeable ethnologists. Powell's foreword, which did draw on some of the material in Corle's letter, appeared in 1955.

7. Edwin Corle, *Fig Tree John* (New York: Liveright, 1935), p. 6. All quotations are from the widely accessible Liveright reissue of 1971. The original (1935) edition was also published by Liveright, and since the same plates were used in both editions, with only the pagination changed, page references to the original edition can be found by adding the number eight to the references I give to the 1971 edition. Thus, p. 6 in the 1971 edition is the same as p. 14 in the 1935 edition.

8. *Ibid.,* p. 92.

9. *Ibid.,* p. 236.

10. J. Smeaton Chase, *California Desert Trails* (Boston: Houghton Mifflin, 1919), pp. 181–84, 214.

11. Edwin Corle, "Bank Holiday," in *Mojave: A Book of Stories* (New York: Liveright, 1934), pp. 46–47, 51. In addition to showing Corle's early conception of the character of Fig Tree John, "Bank Holiday" gives us an interesting preview of several other features which were to be developed more maturely in the novel. Tony Gee, for example, the "emerging" Indian who has learned how to read, who has a job on a date ranch and a few dollars in the bank, and who drives a "rattly old Ford," is clearly an early study of the Johnny Mack of the novel. Similarly, "Bank Holiday" shows Corle's early — and not entirely successful — probing of what he thought of as the primitive mind. Corle speaks, for example, of Tom Lobo's "unimaginative mind" and of John Whitewater's having "no creative imagination." All in all, these men come off sounding rather stupidly cave-mannish in their reactions to the closing of the bank. Traces of this attitude toward the mental workings of primitive men can still be found a year later in the novel, but by the time Corle wrote the more extended work, he had outgrown much of his penchant for underestimating the potentialities of "the Indian mind."

12. *Fig Tree John*, p. 198.

13. *Ibid.*, p. 47.

14. *Ibid.*, p. 162.

15. *Ibid.*, p. 59.

16. *Ibid.*, p. 56.

17. Letter from Special Commissioner Terrell to Fig Tree John, March 28, 1917; reprinted in Part One.

18. *Fig Tree John*, p. 16.

19. *Ibid.*, p. 17.

20. Quotations from "Bank Holiday" are all from p. 46; from the novel all from pp. 5 and 237.

21. *Fig Tree John*, p. 234.

22. Albert B. Reagan, *Notes on the Indians of the Fort Apache Region*, Anthropological Papers of the American Museum of Natural History, vol. 30, pt. 5 (New York: American Museum of Natural History, 1930), pp. 281–345.

23. Pliny Earle Goddard, *Myths and Tales from the White Mountain Apache*, Anthropological Papers of the American Museum of Natural History, vol. 24, pt. 2 (New York: American Museum of Natural History, 1919), pp. 87–139.

24. John C. Cremony, *Life Among the Apaches* (San Francisco: A. Roman & Company, 1868).

25. John G. Bourke, *On the Border with Crook* (New York: Charles Scribner's Sons, 1891).

26. John G. Bourke, *The Medicine-Men of the Apache*, Ninth Annual Report of the Bureau of Ethnology to the Secretary of the Smithsonian Institution (Washington: Government Printing Office, 1892), pp. 443–603.

27. Frederick Webb Hodge, *Handbook of American Indians*, Smithsonian Institution, Bureau of American Ethnology Bulletin 30 (Washington: Government Printing Office, 1912).

28. Goddard, p. 103.
29. Bourke, *On the Border,* p. 219, and *Medicine-Men,* p. 465. In both cases the Apache form of the name is given as *Chaundezi.*
30. *Fig Tree John,* p. 52.
31. Cremony, p. 243. See also Goddard, p. 103, n. 1; Bourke, *On the Border,* p. 131; and Bourke, *Medicine-Men,* p. 461.
32. *Fig Tree John,* p. 57.
33. *Ibid.,* p. 43.
34. Bourke, *On the Border,* p. 131. See also Reagan, pp. 291–95.
35. *Fig Tree John,* p. 32.
36. Reagan, p. 295. See also Hodge, p. 66. It is interesting that, whereas Reagan later mentions a taboo against killing or even touching snakes (p. 306), Corle has Agocho speak of them as "very fine food" (p. 34). Either Corle missed Reagan's reference to snakes, or else he chose to ignore it in favor of using what would in 1935 have been a "shocking" detail showing how primitive these Apaches were.
37. Reagan, p. 298.
38. *Ibid.,* p. 291.
39. *Ibid.,* p. 298.
40. *Ibid.,* p. 290.
41. *Fig Tree John,* p. 32.
42. Reagan, p. 291.
43. *Fig Tree John,* p. 27.
44. Bourke, *Medicine-Men,* pp. 570–72.
45. Reagan, p. 297.
46. Bourke, *On the Border,* p. 132.
47. Reagan, pp. 311–12.
48. *Ibid.,* p. 307.
49. *Fig Tree John,* p. 37.
50. *Ibid.,* p. 173.
51. Goddard, p. 100, n. 2.
52. See Grenville Goodwin, *Western Apache Raiding and Warfare,* ed. Keith H. Basso (Tucson: University of Arizona Press, 1971), pp. 288–98.
53. *Fig Tree John,* pp. 172–73.
54. Reagan, p. 309.
55. *Ibid.,* p. 311.
56. *Fig Tree John,* p. 174.
57. Reagan, p. 309.
58. *Fig Tree John,* p. 173.
59. Bourke, *Medicine-Men,* p. 507.
60. Reagan, p. 309.
61. *Ibid.,* p. 315.
62. Bourke, *Medicine-Men,* p. 467.
63. Cremony, p. 297.
64. *Fig Tree John,* p. 127.

65. Reagan, p. 315.
66. *Ibid.,* p. 316.
67. *Fig Tree John,* p. 130.
68. Cremony, p. 297.
69. *Fig Tree John,* p. 307.
70. *Ibid.,* p. 15.
71. *Ibid.,* p. 18.
72. *Ibid.,* p. 23.
73. Cremony, p. 85.
74. *Fig Tree John,* p. 41.
75. *Ibid.,* p. 47.
76. *Ibid.,* p. 53.
77. Cremony, p. 187.
78. Reagan, pp. 313–14.
79. *Fig Tree John,* p. 19.
80. *Ibid.,* p. 147.
81. *Ibid.,* p. 234.
82. *Ibid.,* pp. 262–63.
83. Cremony, p. 214.
84. Bourke, *Medicine-Men,* p. 499.
85. Bourke, *On the Border,* p. 133.
86. *Fig Tree John,* p. 32.
87. *Ibid.,* p. 33.
88. *Ibid.,* p. 260.
89. *Ibid.,* p. 112.
90. *Ibid.,* p. 126.
91. *Ibid.,* pp. 140–41.
92. *Ibid.,* p. 143.
93. *Ibid.,* p. 35.
94. *Ibid.*
95. Reagan, p. 301.
96. *Fig Tree John,* p. 251.
97. *Ibid.,* p. 258.
98. Just to set the record straight, Miller is wrong to suggest that it was an "Apache custom" for a man to claim sexual rights to his son's wife (see Miller's introduction to the 1971 Liveright edition of the novel, p. xii). It is true that under certain circumstances Apaches were polygamous, but it was quite improper for an Apache man to sleep with his daughter-in-law. It is important to note that Agocho claims sexual rights to Maria not because she is Johnny Mack's wife, but because in Agocho's view she is *not* his wife. For Agocho, she is just a family chattel, a foreign captive, a slave to be used in common by both of them: "She really wouldn't be N'Chai Chidn's wife, or anybody's wife, but she would be their property to work for them and cook for them and sleep with them. That's all she was good for and she was only a white girl. And when N'Chai Chidn got back to the White River he could have an Apache wife for himself" (*Fig Tree John,* p. 258).

99. *Fig Tree John,* p. 258.

100. John Collier was the Commissioner of Indian Affairs who was responsible for drafting the Indian Reorganization Act, passed by Congress in 1934, the year Corle was writing *Fig Tree John.* The Act, which provided a "New Deal" for Indian tribes, forbade further sale or allotment of reservation lands, gave to tribes the power to set up their own tribal governments, and encouraged the preservation of traditional Indian ways. It is interesting to note that in Corle's second novel, *People on the Earth* (1937), he shows that following the "white man's way" is not necessarily a satisfactory solution for young Indians.

101. Pilkington, p. 57. Cf. Manfred (note 1 above) who praises the novel for being "a true story about Indians" and "utterly true."

102. Margaret Wallace, review of *Fig Tree John* in *New York Times Book Review,* September 15, 1935, p. 7.

103. James Broughton, review of *Fig Tree John, New York Herald Tribune Books,* September 29, 1935, p. 2.

104. Pilkington, p. 54. Oliver La Farge was a little more accurate when he said that while the Indians in *Fig Tree John* are "real Indians made clear" they nevertheless are "products of the white man's mind" and are "sometimes marked with the author's fingerprints." See his review in *Saturday Review,* 12 (October 26, 1935), p. 11.

105. Pilkington, p. 52.

106. Miller, p. xviii.

107. Broughton, p. 2.

108. Edwin Corle, *Desert Country* (New York: Duell, Sloan, and Pearce, 1941), p. 124. It is interesting to compare this quotation with the statement in the 1953 letter to Powell: Fig Tree John "will never quit; he has to be killed. It's all or nothing, win or lose, victory or death with him."

109. Edwin Corle. *The Gila: River of the Southwest* (New York: Rinehart, 1951), p. 287.

110. *Fig Tree John,* p. 307.

111. Miller, p. ix.

ANNOTATED BIBLIOGRAPHY

Aguilar, Louisa. Interview with author, February 16, 1974.

Anthony, Frances. "Below Sea-Level." *The Land of Sunshine,* 15 (July 1901), pp. 22–26.

Earliest recorded first-person description of a visit to Juanito Razon's camp. Relevant portions reprinted in Part One.

Bailey, Philip A. *Golden Mirages.* New York: Macmillan, 1940.

On pp. 109–10 is a description of a meeting at "Fig Tree John Spring" in the early 1870s. From this account it appears that Juanito Razon knew where there was gold in the hills.

Bean, Lowell John. Letter to author, January 9, 1974.

Bean, Lowell John, and Lawton, Harry W. *A Bibliography of the Cahuilla Indians of California.* Banning, California: Malki Museum Press, 1967.

This 28-page pamphlet lists many works relating to the Cahuilla Indians, including some on Juanito Razon.

―――――. *The Cahuilla Indians of Southern California.* Malki Museum Brochure no. 1. Banning, California: Malki Museum Press, 1965.

A brief but useful discussion of the history, social organization, arts, crafts, and lifeways of the Cahuilla Indians. There is a short passage on Juanito Razon on the next-to-last page.

Bisbee, Melvin. Letter to author, January 17, 1974.

Blake, William P. "Geological Report." *Reports of Explorations and Surveys to Ascertain the Most Practicable and Economical Route for a Railroad from the Mississippi River to the Pacific Ocean.* 33rd. Congress, 2nd. Session, House of Representatives Executive Document no. 91. Washington: A. O. P. Nicholson, Printer, 1856.

On pp. 97–99 is a description of one of the earliest encounters of the white man with the Cahuilla Indians. Juanito Razon is not mentioned by name, but it is quite possible that he might have been present at the meetings described.

Bourke, John G. *The Medicine-Men of the Apache.* Ninth Annual Report of the Bureau of Ethnology to the Secretary of the Smithsonian Institution, pp. 443–603. Washington: Government Printing Office, 1892.

A detailed account of the beliefs and the religious practices of the early Apaches, as observed, recorded, and commented upon by Bourke. Corle almost certainly consulted this work for background materials on Apache customs.

————. *On the Border with Crook.* New York: Charles Scribner's Sons, 1891.

A readable account of Bourke's observations on his assignment in the field with General Crook's troops on duty in the southwest. Contains several pages (see especially pp. 123–35) describing Apaches and their ways. Corle probably consulted it.

Broughton, James. Review of *Fig Tree John. New York Herald Tribune Books,* September 29, 1935, p. 2.

Praises the novel as a "skillful and unusual book, as ironic as it is sympathetic."

Bureau of Indian Affairs. Letters relating to Juanito Razon, 1913–29. On file at the Bureau of Indian Affairs, Southern California Agency, Riverside, California, and at the National Archives, Washington, D.C. (Bureau of Indian Affairs File no. 131113–13, California Special 320).

Most of these letters relate to real estate negotiations made necessary by the fact that Juanito Razon was living on land which had been deeded to the Southern Pacific Railroad. The most important of these letters are reprinted in Part One.

Burns, Helen, *Salton Sea Story.* Palm Desert, California: Desert Magazine Press, 1952.

A brief account on p. 25 describes Juanito Razon's movement from "Fig Tree John Spring" to Agua Dulce when the Salton Sea was formed. According to Burns "he was not popular among the white people."

Carlson, Edith. "The Death Bed Map of a Lost Desert Gold Mine." *Palm Springs Villager,* September 1951, pp. 12–15.

Juanito Razon is mentioned in connection with a lost gold mine near his home in the Santa Rosa Mountains.

Chase, J. Smeaton. *California Desert Trails.* Boston: Houghton Mifflin, 1919.

On pp. 181–83 is a detailed account of Chase's visit to Juanito Razon's camp around 1917. It is of particular interest because Corle probably consulted it before writing his novel. Relevant portions are reprinted in Part Two.

Colley, Nevada C. *From Maine to Mecca.* Indio, California, 1967.
A "fictionalized" account of the life of an early Coachella Valley
pioneer. Several of the incidents have to do with Juanito Razon
(see especially pp. 121–24, 156–58, and 225–26).

Corle, Edwin. *Desert Country.* New York: Duell, Sloan, and Pearce,
1941.
Contains brief descriptions of a number of the southwestern
Indian tribes. In his account of the Apaches (see pp. 119–24)
Corle is eager to correct the "sentimentalized" view of Indians
by mentioning some of the cruel deeds known to have been done
by Apaches.

————. *Fig Tree John.* New York: Liveright, 1935. Reissued 1971
in hardcover and paper editions.
Around 10,000 copies of the various Liveright editions have been
sold. Several editions have been published by other publishers.
Pyramid Books brought out an abridged version in 1952 under
the title *Apache Devil.* Ward Ritchie published a limited edition
in 1955. In 1972 Simon & Schuster brought out a Pocket Book
edition; 90,000 copies have been sold. Tandem-Universal Pub-
lishing Corporation, Ltd., brought out a paperback edition in
England in 1972.

————. *The Gila: River of the Southwest.* New York: Rinehart,
1951.
Contains an interesting historical survey of the Apaches and their
dealings with the white man.

————. Letter to Lawrence Clark Powell, February 18, 1953. Depart-
ment of Special Collections, Research Library, University of
California, Los Angeles.
A valuable account of how and why Corle wrote *Fig Tree John.*
Powell made use of much of this information in his introduction
to the Ward Ritchie limited edition. Letter reprinted in Part
Two.

————. *Mojave: A Book of Stories.* New York: Liveright, 1934.
All of these stories have a desert setting, and several of them
have Indian characters. Of particular interest is "Bank Holiday"
(pp. 43–53), in which a Coachella Valley Indian named Fig
Tree John is mentioned and described briefly.

Cremony, John C. *Life Among the Apaches.* New York: A. Roman
& Company, 1868.
An opinionated report by a United States soldier who had encoun-
tered Apaches while he was on duty in the Southwest. Corle prob-
ably relied on this early work for some of his impressions of
Apache life and character.

Davis, Edward H. *Edward H. Davis and the Indians of the South-western United States and Northwest Mexico.* Edited by Charles Russell Quinn and Elena Quinn. Downey, California: Elena Quinn, Publisher, 1965.

Contains a brief description (p. 112) of Juanito Razon, whom Davis sat next to at an Indian funeral in 1917.

Desert Barnacle and Coachella Valley Submarine, October 29, 1949, p. 10.

Under the headline, "Fig Tree John was Best Known Indian in Early Days Here," this very brief newspaper article says nothing new about Juanito Razon except perhaps that he was a "beloved" resident of the Coachella Valley.

Ewers, Retta E. "Fig Tree John." *Palm Springs Villager,* February 1953, p. 24. Reprinted with small changes in phrasing as "Fig Tree John Was a Bluffer" in *Desert Magazine,* 30 (March 1967), pp. 6–7.

Basing her account largely on the Shumway and Yost article, Ewers adds a few original observations and interpretations.

Foulkes, Cecelia. Letter to author, January 20, 1974.

Gifford, Edward Winslow. *Clans and Moieties in Southern California.* University of California Publications in American Archaeology and Ethnology, vol. 14, no. 2, pp. 155–219. Berkeley: University of California Press, 1918.

Lists Juanito Razon on p. 191 as belonging to the Palkausinakela Clan of the Cahuilla Wild Cat Moiety. Strong, p. 49, corrects the name of the clan.

Goddard, Pliny Earle. *Myths and Tales from the White Mountain Apache.* Anthropological Papers of the American Museum of Natural History, vol. 24, pt. 2, pp. 87–139. New York: American Museum of Natural History, 1919.

A translation of several Apache myths and stories. Corle probably consulted especially the "Creation Myth" for ideas about Ste-na-tlih-a and her two sons.

Grant, Ulysses S., IV. "A Midsummer Motoring Trip." *Historical Society of Southern California Quarterly,* 43 (March 1961), pp. 85–96. Excerpts reprinted in *Desert Magazine,* 25 (March 1962), pp. 20–21, 43–44.

Describes how Juanito Razon helped to rescue Grant and his brother when their car broke down in the desert in 1913. Relevant portions reprinted in Part One.

Heintzelman, S. P. Report to E. D. Townsend on Southern California Indians, July 15, 1853. 34th Congress, 3rd Session. House of Representatives Executive Document no. 76, Serial no. 906, pp. 34–58. Washington: Government Printing Office, 1857.

Mentions a meeting with "Razon's People" near the Salton Sink (dry basin) in 1851.

Hilton, John. "Paradise for Hammer Hounds." *Desert Magazine,* 5 (January 1942), pp. 18–21.

After an unsuccessful attempt to locate the "legendary lost mine of Fig Tree John," Hilton concludes that there probably was no such mine.

Hodge, Frederick Webb. *Handbook of American Indians.* Smithsonian Institution, Bureau of American Ethnology Bulletin 30. 2 vols. Washington: Government Printing Office, 1912.

This work contains a brief summary (vol. 1, pp. 63–67) of the history and some of the customs of Apaches. Corle knew Hodge and would surely have consulted this book.

Hughes, Tom. *History of Banning and San Gorgonio Pass.* Banning, California: Banning Record Print, 1938.

Contains several brief notices about Juanito Razon and his family, culled mainly from local newspapers. In 1914 there was reference to a "legend" that the old man "had not smiled since his squaw died 50 years before" (p. 48), and in 1927 a notice of his death reported that he was buried in his army coat and top hat (pp. 55–57).

Imperial Irrigation District News, 32 (March–April 1971), pp. 3–4.

A brief biographical sketch based largely on the Shumway and Yost article. An original portion recounts Ben Laflin's recollection of the time in 1912 when Juanito Razon came to M. K. White's store in Thermal (several miles north of Mecca) complaining, chiefly by means of gestures, of being sick. Laflin guessed from the gestures that the Indian was constipated and suggested that White sell him some castor oil: "And castor oil was indeed what Fig Tree John needed. White gave him a bottle, John handed him a few coins and departed, happily grunting to himself."

James, George Wharton. *The Wonders of the Colorado Desert.* 2 vols. Boston: Little, Brown, 1907.

Contains a one-paragraph description (vol. 1, pp. 251–52) of Juanito Razon's home and fig trees, based largely on Jocie Wallace's article.

James, Harry C. *The Cahuilla Indians.* Los Angeles: Westernlore Press, 1960. Reprinted 1969 by Malki Museum Press.

Contains a useful chapter on Juanito Razon (pp. 129–33), much of it derived from the Shumway and Yost article.

———. "Fig Tree John." *True West,* June 1961, pp. 18, 49.

Covers much of the same information that appeared in *The Cahuilla Indians* (above).

————. "The Many Springs of Fig Tree John." *Palm Springs Life,* 3 (March 22, 1961), pp. 44–47.

Briefly outlines Juanito Razon's move to "Fig Tree John Spring" in the 1870s and then to Agua Dulce after the rising Salton Sea forced him to move to higher ground.

Kroeber, A. L. *Handbook of the Indians of California.* Smithsonian Institution, Bureau of American Ethnology Bulletin 78. Washington: Government Printing Office, 1925.

A brief historical and ethnographic sketch of the Cahuilla Indians appears on pp. 692–708. Juanito Razon is mentioned on p. 706 as being a member of the Palkausinakela Clan of the Wild Cat Moiety. This last is corrected by Strong, p. 49.

La Farge, Oliver, Review of *Fig Tree John. Saturday Review,* 12 (October 26, 1935), p. 11.

A generally favorable review of Corle's novel, which had appeared not long after the reviewer's own *Laughing Boy,* another important novel about Indians.

Lawson, S. S. Report to Commissioner of Indian Affairs, August 20, 1881. *Annual Report of the Commissioner of Indian Affairs to the Secretary of the Interior for the Year 1881,* pp. 13–15. Washington: Government Printing Office, 1881.

On p. 14 is an account of the difficulties arising because of the allocation of odd-numbered sections to the Southern Pacific Railroad Company.

Littlefield, W. M. *Hydrology and Physiography of the Salton Sea, California.* Hydrologic Investigations, HA 222. Washington: United States Geological Survey, 1966.

This map with text shows the variations in the level of the Salton Sea in recent history and discusses some of the past history of the area, including the nature of "Lake Cahuilla," an ancient lake or bay. The waterline of this old lake is still visible 200 feet up on the slopes of the Santa Rosa Mountains.

McCarroll, June A. W. "Fig Tree John's Uniform." *Desert Magazine,* 4 (October 1941), p. 2.

This letter to the editor helps to establish the source of one of Juanito Razon's army coats and silk top hats.

Manfred, Frederick. Review in *Minneapolis Tribune,* May 23, 1971, p. E9.

A very sympathetic review published at the time of the Liveright reissue of 1971: "beautifully written," "a true story about Indians," "a great book."

Marshall, H. E. "Peg Leg Gold Secret Hidden with Fig Tree John in Death." As told to W. A. Linkletter. *Palm Springs Villager,* March 1955, pp. 16–17, 42.

An apparently authentic account by Marshall of his experiences with the famous prospector, Pegleg Smith. Smith told Marshall that Juanito Razon was his partner or assistant in a gold mine venture in the Santa Rosa Mountains. Portions reprinted in Part One.

Miller, Walter James. "Edwin Corle and the American Dilemma." Introduction to the Liveright reissue of *Fig Tree John*, pp. ix–xviii. New York: Liveright, 1971.

A generally sound discussion of the novel, emphasizing both its literary excellence and its ecological relevance to today's world.

Moore, Mrs. Otho. Letter to author, January 24, 1974.

[Nordland, Ole J.] "Fig Tree John, Proud Early Resident." In *Coachella Valley's Golden Years*, p. 34. Indio, California: Coachella Valley County Water District, 1968.

A half-page biographical sketch based largely on the Shumway and Yost article.

Penn, Jane. Interview with author, February 15, 1974.

Pilkington, William T. "Edwin Corle and the Southwestern Indian." *Western Review*, 4 (Winter 1967), pp. 51–57. Reprinted in Pilkington's book, *My Blood's Country: Studies in Southwestern Literature*, pp. 39–49. Fort Worth: Texas Christian University Press, 1973.

A review of most of Corle's fiction, lamenting the fact that it was largely neglected after Corle's death. Pilkington especially praises *Fig Tree John* ("the finest novel about an Indian" ever published) and *People on the Earth* (1937), Corle's second novel.

Powell, Lawrence Clark. "The Southwest and Edwin Corle." Foreword to the Ward Ritchie limited edition of *Fig Tree John*, pp. 3–7. Los Angeles: Ward Ritchie, 1955.

A sympathetic discussion of *Fig Tree John* and the region and traditions which helped to shape it. Some of the information it contains came from Corle's 1953 letter to his friend.

Reagan, Albert B. *Notes on the Indians of the Fort Apache Region.* Anthropological Papers of the American Museum of Natural History, vol. 31, pt. 5, pp. 280–345. New York: American Museum of Natural History, 1930.

A remarkably complete and informative discussion of many aspects of the life and customs of the White Mountain Apaches. Corle relied more on Reagan's account than on any other for his ethnographic material on Apaches.

Riverside Press-Enterprise. November 16, 1958, p. C–12.

A lengthy and unusually complete newspaper article based largely on the Shumway and Yost article.

Rust, Horatio N. Letter to Commissioner of Indian Affairs, May 13, 1892. 52nd Congress, 1st Session. Senate Executive Document no. 108, pp. 5–6. Washington: Government Printing Office, 1892.

Describes how an unnamed Cahuilla "captain" had set up posts across a road to keep certain Indians out of certain fields. The man described may not be Juanito Razon, but this letter may explain certain of his misunderstood actions.

San Bernardino Sun. October 9, 1906.

Under a headline which reads, "Indian Agent Says Razon Dreamed," this newspaper article describes Juanito Razon's displacement by the rising Salton Sea. Reprinted in Part One.

Shumway, Nina Paul. *Your Desert and Mine.* Los Angeles: Westernlore Press, 1960.

Mrs. Shumway's father was the model for the "Mr. Paul" in Corle's novel. On pp. 39–41 of her book about pioneer date ranching in the desert, she discusses her contacts with Juanito Razon.

Shumway, Nina Paul, and Yost, Leland. "Fig Tree John's Gun Was Never Loaded." *Desert Magazine,* 4 (January 1941), pp. 5–7.

The most complete and influential account of the life and doings of Juanito Razon, written by two early Coachella Valley residents who knew him as a caller at their ranches. The article was written in part to "set the record straight" after the appearance of Corle's biographically inaccurate novel about Fig Tree John. Reprinted in Part Two.

Strong, William Duncan. *Aboriginal Society in Southern California.* University of California Publications in American Archaeology and Ethnology, vol. 26. Berkeley: University of California Press, 1929.

Identifies Juanito Razon's clan and discusses when it migrated to "Fig Tree John Spring" (see especially pp. 49, 81).

Taylor, Jack R. Letter to author, February 4, 1974.

Twentieth Century Authors, First Supplement. Edited by Stanley J. Kunitz. New York: H. W. Wilson, 1955.

On pp. 230–31 is a brief autobiographical sketch by Corle about his youth, his education, his literary apprenticeship, and his books.

Wallace, Jocie. "On the Desert." *The Youth's Instructor,* October 17, 1905, p. 2.

An account of a visit to Juanito Razon's camp in 1905. Portions reprinted in Part One.

Wallace, Margaret. Review of *Fig Tree John. New York Times Book Review,* September 15, 1935, pp. 7, 18.

Praises the novel as one with "plenty of substance" and one which successfully probes a "primitive mind."

Werner, Louise T. "We Climbed Rabbit Peak." *Desert Magazine*, 15 (September 1952), pp. 16–19.

Contains several paragraphs on Juanito Razon, most of them deriving from the article by Shumway and Yost. Werner adds a story about how the old Indian may have been responsible for the death of a prospector who got too close to Juanito Razon's gold mine.

INDEX